# Synapses, Circuits, and the Beginnings of Memory

The Cognitive Neuroscience Institute Monograph Series
Michael S. Gazzaniga, editor

Gary Lynch. *Synapses, Circuits, and the Beginnings of Memory* (with commentaries by Gordon M. Shepherd, Ira B. Black, and Herbert P. Killackey), 1986

# Synapses, Circuits, and the Beginnings of Memory

Gary Lynch

with commentaries by
Gordon M. Shepherd,
Ira B. Black, and
Herbert P. Killackey

**A Bradford Book**
The MIT Press
Cambridge, Massachusetts
London, England

*Second printing, 1987*

© 1986 by The Massachusetts Institute of Technology

*Printed in the United States of America by Edwards Brothers.*

Library of Congress Cataloging-in-Publication Data

Lynch, Gary.
  Synapses, circuits, and the beginnings of memory.

  (The Cognitive Neuroscience Institute monograph series)
  Based on a paper presented at the Conference of the Cognitive Neuroscience Institute, July 1984.
  "A Bradford book."
  Includes bibliographies.
  1. Memory—Physiological aspects—Addresses, essays, lectures. 2. Synapses—Addresses, essays, lectures. 3. Neural circuitry—Addresses, essays, lectures. I. Shepherd, Gordon M., 1933–.II. Black, Ira B. III. Killackey, Herbert P. IV. Title. V. Series. [DNLM: 1. Memory—physiology.
  2. Neurons—physiology. 3. Synapses—physiology.
  WL 102 L987s]
  QP406.L96  1986      153.1'2      85-28357
  ISBN 0-262-12114-X

# Contents

# Introduction

This monograph, based on a paper by Gary Lynch and commentaries on it by three participants at the Conference of the Cognitive Neuroscience Institute, July 1984, represents an effort to articulate how neurobiologic discoveries can be interpreted in terms of psychological memory. Gary Lynch summarizes findings in both the biochemical and physiological responses of brain areas known to be involved in memory. He also uses his ideas on evolutionary theory as a basis for constructing a model of how cellular processes might be responsible for storing psychological memory. Gordon Shepherd addresses how a particular cortical cell system, the apical dendrites of cortical pyramidal cells, could be active in storing information. In addition, Ira Black discusses how individual neurons undergo their own mutability, and how this must be taken into account in modeling the way neural cells support mnemonic processes. Last, a general discussion of the conference, composed of comments made by the meeting participants, is summarized by Herbert Killackey.

In considering these papers it is helpful to consider briefly some of the background in memory research. Twenty-five years ago, the neuron was regarded as the basic element of the brain, and it was believed that neurons interact in an undefined way to store information (Hebb, 1949; Lashley, 1950). Information was stored in "engrams," and scientists vigorously sought to identify their location in the brain. It was suggested that information might be retrieved as the result of certain neural pathways developing relations that found them responding more readily to a specific input. Again, how this was actually accomplished was not well articulated. What became firmly established in the minds of investigators was that something changed at the most elemental level, the neuron, that was responsible for the storage of information. While the big "where" in the brain was never identified, the little "where" of the neuron as being the prime candidate became ingrained in the brain sciences (Kandel and Schwartz, 1982). This view, which is the current view of most neurobiologists, was best supported in vertebrates by studies of the cellular mechanisms of the hippocampus, a structure thought to be involved in memory (Lynch, this volume).

The hippocampus was implicated in human memory after the hippocampi were removed in a young man in an effort to control epilepsy (Milner, 1959). This patient, the famous Case H.M., experienced an incredible mental change, the gist of which was that new information was very difficult to remember, whereas old memories remained largely intact. There was something about the absence of the hippocampus that impaired the brain's ability to lay down new information in long-term memory. This was a very exciting observation for many reasons, not the least of which was that it underscored the many stages through which information must pass before it is biologically recorded.

Armed with this insight, the cellular neurobiologist began to study the hippocampus in detail. Curiously, from the point of view of experimental cell biology, the hippocampus was selected for study more for its surgical accessibility and its elegant and orderly anatomy than because of the lesion effects reported in humans. Since memories prior to surgery remain intact in such patients, hippocampal lesions only effect the storage of new information. Consequently, the hippocampus is not the place to look for where memories are stored. Nonetheless, one very ingenious scientist, Gary Lynch, figured out a way to remove a slice of a rat hippocampus and place it into tissue culture for micro-inspection. Using small electrodes he was able to show that certain hippocampal neurons could be stimulated in such a way that other postsynaptic neurons permanently changed their pattern of responding. After years of postulating that neuronal interactions of this sort occurred, one such interaction had finally been identified that could be part of the cellular basis of long-term memory. The assumption of neurobiologists that plastic changes occur at the level of a single synapse had been partially realized. Yet, soon after this accomplishment, the question addressed by neurobiologists seemed to change.

When this elegant study and other studies on single-synapse systems are considered together, it seems clear that the time has come to recognize that a major categorical error has been made by neurobiologists interested in the problem of memory. Consider the professor showing the new student around campus. The professor points out the chemistry building, the physics building, the biology building, the humanities building, the gymnasium, and so on. The student takes it all in and then finally asks, "This is all fine, but where is the university?" A similar question can be asked about the study of memory. Here, the neurobiologist has come to assume that "memory" is the product of a synapse, when in fact it is likely to be a systems property emerging out of thousands of synaptic processes.

Scientists working in the field of memory are trying to solve one of the most difficult problems of the mind. In my estimation, neurobiologists have chosen to study memory as they do, not because their approach bears directly on the problem, but because up until recently it has been as close as one can get to the problem, given both the way memory has been characterized and the technological tools available for research. While great knowledge has been gained, the first true challenge is to structure the neurobiologic question in a way that reflects psychological processes. In order to do this, one must first consider how the human memory process operates.

Even the most cursory review of our knowledge of psychological memory would suggest that the complete understanding of a single synaptic system is of limited utility. Just as no one would argue that a complete knowledge of the physical properties of a single transistor would in any way reveal how "information" is represented in a computer, so it also goes for the brain. The new charge to the neurobiologist arising out of cognitive science must be to understand the function of neural networks. Consider the following.

One of the major advances of cognitive science in the past few years has been to show how cognitive processes such as memory can be broken down into component operations than need not share a common brain region. It is no longer viable to think of a memory as a monolithic function that is instantiated at a unique site in the nervous system. Information impinges on an organism under a variety of internal states, at varying times, places, affective states, alertness, and a host of other dimensions that have been ignored in the past (Gazzaniga, 1984). Each experience that is recorded in the brain has all of these dimensions associated with the event in question.

This realization of the network aspect of memory found support from studies of patients with specific pathologies, pathologies that may disrupt specific aspects of a memory, while leaving others unaffected. Hence a patient may lose the capacity to remember the time of a particular event but not its place (Hirst and Volpe, 1984). Dissociations like this suggest that in human memory there are several superordinate organizing systems active in the tagging of all new information. Memory for a prior event is stored in relation to all of these other factors. If one of these other systems is not functioning, new information may be stored, but in an impoverished state. As a consequence, recall suffers. Some of the cues that automatically exist in the normal brain to assist in locating previously stored information are unavailable, and as a result accessing the information is difficult.

To summarize, it is observations of this sort that urge the view that information storage in the nervous system is more a systems property of neural networks than a property of synapses per se. It is inconceivable that a single synaptic site could encode such a vast array of complex information. If this view is correct, the question regarding memory becomes one of understanding how the storage of information is distributed throughout a neural network, a network of active synaptic sites.

In this volume an attempt is made to understand the synapse in a larger framework. It is the result of a conference held in Moorea, where the incomparable beauty of the South Seas reminded all participants how sublimely complicated is the problem of memory. We are indebted to Lynch for his remarkable effort.

This monograph is the first of a series to be published under the auspices of the Cognitive Neuroscience Institute. The Institute holds one meeting per year. The aim of each meeting is to discuss critical issues in the brain and behavioral sciences, issues that draw attention to the complex problem of relating neurobiologic processes to psychological phenomena. All too frequently investigators working at one level of inquiry fail to produce models that incorporate the constraints and realities of another level. Our meetings strive to enlighten all on this profound problem.

Michael S. Gazzaniga, Director
The Cognitive Neuroscience Institute
New York, New York

## References

Gazzaniga, M. S. Advances in cognitive neurosciences: the problem of information storage in the human brain. In J. L. McGaugh, G. Lynch, and N. M. Weinberger (eds.), *Neurobiology of Learning and Memory*. New York: Guilford Press, 1984.

Hebb, D. O. *Organization of Behavior*. New York: Wiley, 1949.

Hirst, W., and Volpe, B. Automatic and effortful encoding in amnesia. In *Handbook of Cognitive Neuroscience* (M. Gazzaniga, ed.), New York: Plenum Press, 1984, pp. 369–386.

Kandel, E., and Schwartz, J. Molecular biology of memory: modulation of transmitter release. *Science* 218:433–443, 1982.

Lashley, K. In search of the engram. *Symposium of the Society for Experimental Biology* 4:454–482, 1950.

Lynch, G. This volume.

Milner, B. The memory defect in bilateral hippocampal lesions. *Psychiatric Research Reports* 11:43–52, 1959.

# Synapses, Circuits, and the Beginnings of Memory

# Synapses, Circuits, and the Beginnings of Memory

## Gary Lynch

---

*Introduction*

Even a partial understanding of the neurobiological processes involved in memory storage would have a major impact on the cognitive sciences. Regional analyses of the mechanism would tell us whether memory is ubiquitous to neuronal and hence behavioral operations or, as in the common computer metaphor, it is localized to particular regions and is called upon and used as needed by planning and coordinating components of the brain. One also suspects that information about the nature of cellular encoding of experience will substantially affect discussion about the duration of memory and the role of rehearsal in maintaining it. Equally significant, the neurobiological data will allow us to address the problem of whether memory as seen in humans is due to the use, in exceedingly complex circuitries, of simple cellular processes common to a broad range of animals or instead reflects novel chemistries that emerged with the higher vertebrates. From this we may be able to decide about the role of conditional associations as found in all vertebrates (and perhaps invertebrates as well) in the formation of bits of memory in humans.

However, as important as they undoubtedly would be, cellular explanations would offer only limited help in unraveling the role of memory in higher "cognitive" behaviors (Gazzaniga, 1983). For this, one would need to place the postulated memory chemistry in the larger context of the circuitries and physiologies of those brain regions thought to be involved in the various aspects of learning and memory.

The problem with doing this is all too apparent; the relevant brain areas are found in the telencephalon, an object of extraordinary and intimidating complexity, and one that is hardly appropriate territory for the application of the analytical techniques of cellular neurobiology.

This has led some to investigate simple forms of learning in the lower regions of the brain or in animals with comparatively simple nervous systems. While impressive gains have been realized from this strategy (for reviews, see Kandel and Schwartz, 1982; Thompson et al., 1984), the problem of whether these models provide a realistic picture of the operating characteristics of mammalian cortex and the memory it produces remains unanswered. The present paper suggests a very different approach to reconnoitering the no-man's-land between the neurosciences and human memory.

Prompted by questions of how to build "thinking" machines, as well as by the computational power offered by modern computers, a number of theorists have developed models of the types of circuitries used by the human brain to accomplish its functions. These models, unrealistic as they are recognized to be, do serve to identify circuit characteristics that are logically dictated by readily apparent parameters of cognition. This confronts the neuroscientist with the question of whether circuitries that correspond to those in the models are actually found in the brain and, if so, whether there are examples in laboratory animals that are sufficiently simple that they can be studied with physiological, chemical, etc., techniques. I shall argue that the answer to both these questions is yes. The point will also be made that recent neurobiological studies have identified forms of synaptic plasticity that are particularly appropriate for both modifying "cognition" networks and producing memory. Much of the present paper will be taken up by a consideration of what can be expected to happen when plasticity of this type is added to brain circuits and in particular whether the behaviors predicted to emerge have features resembling those of human memory.

It will be helpful to summarize the chain of arguments that will be presented.

First, synapses in the hippocampus, cortex, and possibly other brain regions possess the plasticity required for memory storage; a specific biochemical process involving a proteolytic enzyme will be described and proposed as the substrate of some but not all types of memory.

Second, having described a possible cellular mechanism for storage, the paper will consider how it is used by neuronal circuits to produce memory. A number of theorists have argued that memory is encoded in combinatorial circuitries in which inputs carrying disparate types of information converge almost at random in the dendrites of target cells. Using well-established allometric relationships between brain size, neuron density, and dendritic length, I shall argue that circuitries in cerebral cortex, and probably elsewhere in the forebrain, do in fact incorporate a strong combinatorial principle. An attempt will then be made to use data from comparative anatomy and evolutionary history of the telencephalon to deduce the types of combinatorial circuitries that should be found in mammalian cortex and related structures.

Third, the operation of combinatorial circuitries, particularly as they relate to memory, will be considered. Olfaction will be used for this purpose for three reasons:

- olfactory projections into the telencephalon provide an unusually clear example of combinatorial design;
- the modality has direct and well-defined connections with subcortical structures that play a prominent role in human memory; and
- lesions to these subcortical zones produce effects on olfactory memory that closely resemble human amnesia.

Fourth, the effects of adding synaptic plasticity of the type described in the first section of the paper to olfactory circuits will be considered. The position will be taken that plasticity is used to produce stable representations of stimuli and that this provides for recognition memory. Memory thus has its beginnings as a product of an active perceptual process. Higher stages of the system carrying out similar operations will be postulated to produce association and recall.

## I Synaptic Plasticity and Memory Formation

The question of which components of the neuron are responsible for storage is vital to attempts to develop generalized hypotheses about how the brain encodes and makes use of memory. Since individual neurons receive and generate thousands of connections and hence participate in what must be a vast array of potential circuits, most theorists have postulated a central role for synaptic modifications in memory storage. To do otherwise (e.g., to assume that whole cell changes are involved) would impose severe limits on both the capacity and the selectivity of the memory system. All of this requires synapses to possess some rather remarkable properties, and, as will be discussed, recent studies have found that physiological events can indeed alter the structure and function of brain connections. To go further and answer questions about how, when, and where synaptic function is changed in complex neural networks, to say nothing of linking it to particular aspects of memory, will require an understanding of the chemistries that produce it. Accordingly, this first section also reviews experiments on an enzymatic process that is capable of producing stable changes in synapses and briefly describes some first attempts to test for its involvement in memory storage.

A *Physiological Activity Can Modify Synaptic Physiology, Anatomy, and Chemistry*

Starting with the reports by Bliss and his coworkers (Bliss and Gardner-Medwin, 1973; Bliss and Lomo, 1973), many experiments have shown that brief periods ($<1$ sec) of high-frequency axonal stimulation in the hippocampus produce an increase in the strength of synaptic responses that can last anywhere from days to months (e.g., Douglas and Goddard, 1975; Douglas, 1977; Barnes, 1979; for reviews, see Eccles, 1983; Lynch and Baudry, 1984; Seifert, 1983; Voronin, 1983).

A great deal of work has been directed at this long-term potentiation (or LTP) effect, and while many issues remain unresolved, a number of its important characteristics have been determined, among which are the following:

- *Selectivity*   Induction of LTP in one set of afferents to a particular dendritic zone does not produce potentiation in a second input to precisely the same field (Dunwiddie and Lynch, 1978), a result that has been replicated using two afferents to the dendritic tree of a single neuron (Andersen et al., 1980; Barrionuevo and Brown, 1983).
- *Cooperativity*   LTP is larger and more reliably elicited by high-frequency stimulation delivered to a group of axons generating overlapping synaptic fields than when small numbers of fibers are stimulated (McNaughton, Douglas, and Goddard, 1978; Lee, 1982; Barrionuevo and Brown, 1983). It is likely that the induction of the effect depends upon some type of cooperativity between several synapses.
- *Different Forms*   There is reason to suspect that different forms of long-term potentiation with different substrates exist. Racine and coworkers (Racine and Milgram, 1983; Racine, Milgram, and Hafner, 1983) have shown that the high-frequency trains are followed by two types of potentiation, one that decays with a half-life of several hours (LTP1) and a second with a half-life of several days (LTP2); Racine has also found that the induction of seizure proneness ("kindling") in the hippocampus prevents subsequent expression of the longer but not the shorter form of LTP, a result that suggests that these effects are supported by different processes. As mentioned, there have been reports of potentiation lasting for weeks (Bliss and Gardner-Medwin, 1973; Barnes, 1979), and we have recently identified stimulation conditions that produce LTP that is stable for at least a month (Staubli, Roman, and Lynch, 1985). The relationship of the two forms of decremental potentiation described by Racine, or the facilitations of varying duration

found outside the central nervous system (e.g., Brown and McAfee, 1982), to the more persistent variety of LTP, which is presumably of most interest in memory research, is not at all certain. In any event, it is likely that the term "LTP" is being used today to describe different effects, a point that may explain some of the confusion in the literature.

- *Cumulative Nature*    LTP is not an all-or-none effect in that, up to a point, successive episodes of high-frequency stimulation produce increasing amounts of synaptic facilitation (e.g., Bliss and Gardner-Medwin, 1973; Barnes, 1979).
- *Regional Distribution*    Long-term potentiation is not restricted to the hippocampus and can be elicited in the cortex (Lee, 1982), a variety of sites throughout the telencephalon (Racine, Milgram, and Hafner, 1983), and possibly elsewhere in the central and peripheral nervous systems. It should be emphasized that we do not know if the potentiations found in these various systems represent the same phenomenon. The properties listed here have been established in the hippocampus, and there is reason to suspect that some "LTP" effects seen elsewhere have different characteristics (see above).

A substantial body of data indicates that some aspects of LTP are due to changes in the postsynaptic neurons (Dunwiddie, Madison, and Lynch, 1978; Douglas, Goddard, and Riives, 1982; Wigstrom and Gustafsson, 1983; see Bliss and Dolphin, 1984, for an opposing argument). Figure 1 describes one study directed to this issue. Earlier work showed that the probability of inducing LTP as well as its magnitude once elicited were dependent upon extracellular calcium levels (Dunwiddie and Lynch, 1979; Wigstrom, Swann, and Andersen, 1979). In the experiment described in the figure, the calcium chelator EGTA was injected into individual neurons and attempts were made to produce long-term potentiation of synaptic potentials. Other than blocking calcium-mediated after-potentials, EGTA had little effect on the basic physiology of the neurons or their synaptic potentials, but it did greatly reduce the likelihood of eliciting LTP (Lynch et al., 1983).

The postsynaptic change responsible for LTP must be very restricted in an anatomical sense, for, as described immediately above, the induction of LTP in one set of synapses does not result in potentiation of neighboring contacts. Together these findings indicate that the substrates of the potentiation are very likely to be found in the immediate vicinity of the postsynaptic zone.

The idea that the dendritic side of the synaptic complex can be substantially modified by even very brief periods of physiological activity

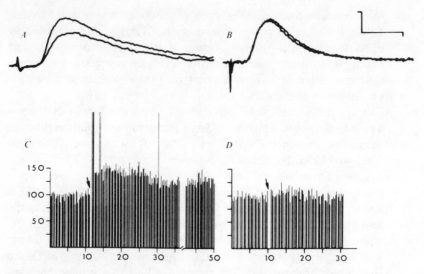

Figure 1
(A) Intracellular recording with a regular electrode. Each trace is the average of six successive responses 10 sec apart collected immediately before and 15 min after five bursts of 300 sec$^{-1}$ stimulation, each lasting 35 msec, delivered through a bipolar electrode in the trajectory of the Schaffer-commissural fibers. Calibration bars: 5 mV and 5 msec for this and subsequent panels. (B) Same as panel (A) except that the neuron was injected with EGTA, a calcium chelator, before the recordings were collected. Note that the cell has a large and stable EPSP but does not exhibit long-term potentiation. (C) Percent change in amplitude of the EPSP after high-frequency stimulation (arrow) for the cell illustrated in (A). The $x$ axis is time in minutes. Each line represents a single response and the average amplitude for the control period is expressed as 100%. The high-amplitude responses are spikes that have been chopped in preparation of the figure. (D) Data for an EGTA filled cell (from Lynch et al., 1983).

has been experimentally confirmed. Probably the clearest evidence is found in a series of ultrastructural studies from my laboratory in which various types of synapses in rat hippocampus were counted and measured following stimulation trains that did or did not produce long-term potentiation. LTP was accompanied by two structural changes: (1) an increase in the number of synapses between axon terminals and main dendritic branches (shaft synapses) and (2) a change in the shape of the dendritic spines (Lee et al., 1980, 1981). Thus synapse formation and spine modification can occur within minutes of a stimulation train that lasts for a fraction of a second. Chang and Greenough (1984) replicated our results and found in addition that the shaft synapse effect was correlated with LTP, that it was stable for at least 8 hr (the longest period tested), and that a population of poorly developed spines ("sessile spines") also increased. Wenzel and Matthies (1985), using chronically implanted rats and high-frequency stimulation of the perforant path, also found a selective increase in shaft synapses and reported that the magnitude of the effect correlated with the degree of synaptic potentiation and was stable for at least 2 days, again the longest time tested. The agreement in results in these independent experiments is striking and provides strong evidence that repetitive synaptic activity produces measurable structural changes, including the formation of new contacts.

As might be expected from these results, high-frequency stimulation episodes leave their mark on the chemistry of the synaptic region. The transmitter used in hippocampal synapses is not firmly established, but a considerable body of indirect evidence points to glutamate, aspartate, or a near relative of these amino acids (for reviews, see DiChiara and Gessa, 1980). We have measured the effects of inducing LTP on "binding sites" thought to form part of the receptor for the endogenous amino acid synaptic transmitter in the hippocampus. The experiments entailed a battery of technical problems, but, as these are described in the original publications and discussed in subsequent reviews, only a summary of the results will be given here: high-frequency stimulation produced an increase in binding sites (Baudry et al., 1980) that was correlated with the occurrence of long-term potentiation (Lynch, Halpain, and Baudry, 1982). Subsequent to this it was reported that intense and repeated bursts of afferent stimulation produce a selective increase in the number of glutamate binding sites in the in situ hippocampus that are very much like those found in our in vitro studies (Savage et al., 1982).

The occurrence of these postsynaptic changes does not rule out a possible presynaptic component to LTP. As noted elsewhere (Lee et al., 1981), changes in shape and ultrastructure of spines might very well produce major reorganizations in the tightly apposed presynaptic terminals. Moreover, the development of new synapses requires changes in afferent fibers. Given the evidence that manipulations of the target neuron can determine whether LTP occurs or not, it is most parsimonious to assume that chemistries in the spine initiate LTP, with the final form of the effect being influenced by alterations in the entire synaptic complex (for a discussion, see Bliss and Dolphin, 1984).

To summarize, physiological stimulation of hippocampal pathways causes lasting specific changes in the physiology, anatomy, and chemistry of synapses, and the latter two effects are correlated with the first. These results offer a plausible substrate of memory storage and tell us that hippocampal synapses must contain a biochemical process that when transiently activated yields long-lasting, functionally significant modifications of the synapse.

B   *A Biochemical Process That Produces Persistent Changes in Synaptic Chemistry and Perhaps Structure*
From the above, we know that high-frequency stimulation increases glutamate binding and potentiates synaptic potentials; we also found that the physiological effect was dependent upon intracellular levels of calcium. This pattern of results points to a testable biochemical prediction, namely, that exposing synapses to calcium should produce an irreversible increase in glutamate receptors. This has been confirmed (Baudry and Lynch, 1979, 1980). The threshold for the effect was about 10 $\mu$M calcium—recent work using calcium sensitive electrodes has shown that intracellular concentrations of the cation are elevated well above this level following repetitive synaptic stimulation (Morris, Krnjevic, and Ropert, 1983). Washing of the synaptic membranes with EGTA after exposure to calcium did not eliminate the added receptors, and so, within the temporal constraints imposed by the biochemical procedures, the elevated binding is irreversible.

Following upon these results, a series of pharmacological and ionic manipulation experiments (Baudry and Lynch, 1980) provided evidence that calcium produced its effects on binding by activating a neutral thiol protease, and in particular an enzyme that has been given the name "calpain" (Murachi et al., 1981a,b). For example, the tripeptide leupeptin, which is a potent inhibitor of calpain (Toy-Oka, Shimuzu, and Masaki, 1978; Aoyagi and Umezawa, 1975), blocks the effects of calcium on glutamate binding. These results have been confirmed and extended in other laboratories (Vargas, Greenbaum, and Costa, 1980).

If a proteolytic enzyme was responsible for the uncovering of receptors, then it would be expected that application of calcium to purified membranes would result in the degradation of proteins in membrane fractions. This was confirmed in experiments in which membranes were incubated with calcium, then dissolved and subjected to polyacrylamide gel electrophoresis. Two prominent high-molecular-weight bands were reduced in the calcium-treated preparations, and this effect was blocked by leupeptin (Baudry et al., 1981). One of these was very likely a subunit of the microtubule-associated proteins (MAPs), which are known to be good substrates for calpain (Sandoval and Weber, 1978), while the other was hypothesized to be "fodrin" (see below).

Calpain is found in the soluble or cytosolic fraction of many cell types—it takes two forms: calpain I with a threshold of 5–30 $\mu$M calcium and calpain II, which is activated at 100–500 $\mu$M calcium (e.g., Mellegren, 1980; Kishomoto et al., 1981; Murachi et al., 1981a,b). The substrates of the protease are high-molecular-weight proteins that are thought to cross-link elements of the cytoskeleton (e.g., microtubule-associated proteins). The enzymes are currently the subject of intensive study because of evidence that they are linked to muscle and nerve degeneration. The finding that enzymes of this type might be involved in regulating receptor numbers in the brain was, to say the least, unexpected.

The calpain hypothesis predicts that the enzyme is associated with crude synaptic membranes, that some protein or proteins in the membranes are substrates for it, and that blocking degradation of the substrates will block the calcium induction of glutamate binding. Recent work by Dr. Robert Siman has satisfied these conditions. Synaptic membranes incubated in low-ionic solutions release calcium sensitive proteolytic activity that by a number of criteria is identical to calpain (Siman, Baudry, and Lynch, 1983); this provided the first evidence that the enzyme is found in a membrane-associated form, a finding now replicated for erythrocytes (Hatanaka et al., 1984). Dr. Siman then coincubated purified calpain with radiolabeled purified fodrin (the protein that was degraded in membranes treated with calcium) and showed that the affinity of the enzyme for this high-molecular-weight protein was comparable to that for the microtubule-associated proteins (Siman, Baudry, and Lynch, 1984). Thus calpain is present in crude synaptic membrane preparations and fodrin is an excellent substrate for it. Fodrin is a member of a family of tetrameric proteins, of which red blood cell spectrin is the archetype, that form a dense coat on the inner face of cell membranes (Hirokawa, Cheney, and Willard, 1983; Levine and Willard, 1981; Lazarides and Nelson, 1982, 1983; Bennett, Davis, and Fowler, 1982; Glenney, Glenney, and Weber, 1982a,b, 1983; Burridge, Kelly, and Mangeat, 1982). Numerous studies have shown that this coat participates in the regulation of the location and motility of transmembrane proteins such as receptors (Levine and Willard, 1983; Marchesi, 1979; Nelson, Colaco, and Lazarides, 1983; Ralston, 1978;

Branton, Cohen, and Teyler, 1981; Goodman and Shiffer, 1983); there is also evidence that the shape of the cell is intimately linked to spectrin-fodrin. Accordingly, the finding that these proteins are excellent substrates for calpain, and that calpain is associated with at least some classes of membranes, provides a novel mechanism by which calcium could regulate the surface chemistry and shape of cell processes such as spines. Finally, antibodies to fodrin block the interaction between calpain and fodrin without inhibiting the enzyme itself; under these conditions, activation of calpain does not result in the appearance of added glutamate binding sites (Siman, Baudry, and Lynch, 1985b). These experiments also demonstrated that addition of the fodrin antibodies *after* calpain had been activated for several minutes had no effect on the induction of binding sites, a result that again illustrates the essentially irreversible nature of calpain's actions.

Studies in other laboratories have shown that fodrin is a major component of highly purified postsynaptic densities (psds); a 140,000-dalton peptide recognized by fodrin antibodies is also present in these preparations (Carlin, Bartlett, and Siekevitz, 1983; Siekevitz, 1985). This protein is almost certainly the breakdown product we demonstrated to result from the proteolysis of synaptosomal membrane fodrin by calpain. It is thus very likely that at least some of the synaptosomal membrane calpain is tightly associated with postsynaptic densities.

Figure 2 collects the above observations into a hypothesis regarding the means by which calcium increases the number of glutamate binding sites in synaptic membranes from the hippocampus and cortex. We postulate that the membrane contains two pools of receptors, one exposed to the extracellular space, the other hidden or blocked. Calcium activates calpain I, which then degrades portions of the fodrin coat and MAP-2 underlying the membrane and thereby exposes some portion of the hidden binding sites.

There is no biochemical technique that would allow us directly to test the idea that calpain is involved in the morphological changes found associated with LTP (e.g., shape change, new synapses—see above). However, studies on red blood cells (RBC) provide evidence that the membrane-associated variant of the enzyme is capable of producing dramatic structural modifications in a rapid and irreversible fashion. When their internal calcium levels are raised, RBCs undergo a transformation in which they convert from concave flat discs (discocytes) into round cells with numerous small extensions ("echinocytes") (White, 1974). Remarkably enough, comparable effects can be elicited in "ghosts," RBCs that have been lysed, emptied of soluble cytoplasmic material, and resealed with added calcium (Palek, Stewart, and Lionetti,

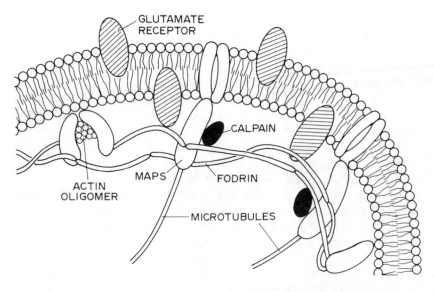

Figure 2

1974). We have found that morphological changes in these ghosts can be elicited by low micromolar levels of internalized calcium and that they are associated with the proteolysis of several membrane proteins including spectrin, all of which are substrates of calpain (Siman, Baudry, and Lynch, 1985a). Moreover, both the proteolysis and morphological transformations are blocked by inhibitors of calpain but not by antagonists of other proteases (Siman, Baudry, and Lynch, 1985a). Recent work from another laboratory (Jinbu et al., 1984) has shown that mild trypsinization of RBCs separates the cytoskeleton from the membrane and causes an irreversible formation of echinocytes. Since the substrates of calpain are thought to cross-link cytoskeleton to membrane, it is conceivable that activation of the enzyme produces structural changes by an analogous action. While one would not like to stress the analogy between RBCs and spines, it is the case that their cytoskeletons have some similarities. Thus they both lack microtubules and perhaps intermediate filaments (Weber et al., 1983), but both appear to have actin filaments (Fifková and Delay, 1982; Landis and Reese, 1983). Spines probably are enriched in the spectrinlike protein fodrin (see above), and a recent report (Kay et al., 1983) suggests the presence in the brain of an analogue of another red blood cell cross-linking protein ("band 3") (see Siman, Baudry, and Lynch, 1985a).

C  *Memory and Synaptic Plasticity: A Hypothesis*
The data described immediately above were used by Michel Baudry and myself to develop a specific hypothesis about the cellular events responsible for storing memory (Lynch and Baudry, 1984).

We assume that the mechanism shown in figure 2 is activated by an influx of calcium (Wong, Prince, and Basbaum, 1979) resulting in an increase in transmitter receptors. Calcium homeostasis is rapidly restored after the burst of synaptic activity, but because the effects of activating the protease (protein breakdown) are irreversible, the added sites remain (figure 3c). This produces a more potent synapse. Note that subsequent episodes of high-frequency activity occur on potentiated synapses, leading to even greater depolarization and hence greater calcium influxes—this could lead to an activation of calpain throughout the spine and neighboring dendritic regions (figure 3d), conditions that would be ideal for producing structural changes. The system could thus be pushed through a sequence from receptor addition to major anatomical reorganization (for a more complete discussion of this hypothesis see Lynch and Baudry, 1984).

Memory is triggered by very brief events, lasts for very long periods, and is strengthened by repetition. There are very good reasons for assuming that at least some versions of it involve selective changes in synapses, a point mentioned earlier and one that will be more fully discussed in a later section. It is also the case that some forms of memory require the simultaneous occurrence of events or cues. The hypothetical mechanism involving calpain, incomplete and overly simplified as it undoubtedly is, accounts for a number of these characteristics, including several that have proved difficult for explanations based on more conventional cell chemistries.

(a) *The process is synaptic and selective.* Its components are contained entirely within an individual spine, and thus allow for changes in specific synapses without modifying neighboring contacts. As will be argued, this is very probably a requirement for a memory mechanism and accords with the pharmacology of LTP.

(b) *It is triggered by a transient event that is physiologically plausible yet not a necessary part of moment-to-moment communication.* Calpain has an absolute requirement for calcium concentrations of 5 $\mu$M or greater, values that might be reached in the spine particularly during prolonged depolarization with correlated extended opening of voltage sensitive calcium channels (if indeed these are present in the spine—Perkel and Perkel, 1985; Robinson and Koch, 1984). Electron microscopic evidence suggesting that spines do accumulate calcium has been reported (Fifková, Markham, and Delay, 1983). It is interesting in this regard that spines lack mitochondria, the only high-capacity calcium

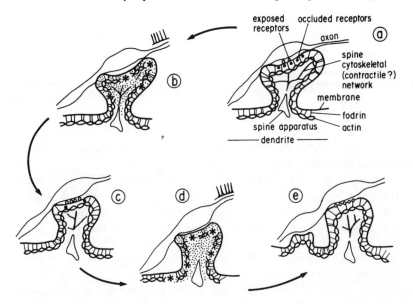

Figure 3
A speculative hypothesis regarding the role of calpain in the production of physiologically induced synaptic plasticity. Panel (a) is a summary of the proposed organization of the dendritic spine "at rest." Note that a polymerized actin network is connected to the plasma membrane by fodrin filaments and that a large pool of membrane receptors is present in the membrane but in a functionally inactive form. In (b), high-frequency stimulation of the axon leads to the release of substantial amounts of transmitter (and possibly other "modulatory" agents), resulting in the opening of calcium channels in the spine and a rise in intracellular calcium. The spine is shown here acting as a calcium trap (see text), resulting in the activation of membrane associated calpain (asterisks). Calpain causes local breakdown of fodrin and other cross-linking proteins, producing a depolymerization of segments of the actin network. Some potential results of this are shown in panel (c). Calcium levels have been restored to normal levels by the operation of intracellular buffering devices and membrane calcium pumps. Because of the irreversible action of calpain, the membrane has become reorganized, exposing the occluded receptors; moreover, the shape of the spine is altered. Together these events result in a more potent synapse. In panel (d), additional bursts of high-frequency activity produce a more pronounced depolarization (because the synapse is potentiated), leading to a still larger influx of calcium. This opens the possibility of calpain activation and perturbations in the dendritic zones surrounding the potentiated spine—the effect illustrated in panel (e) includes the beginning of synapse formation.

buffering element thought to be found in neurons (Blaustein, Ratzlaff, and Schweitzer, 1978); moreover, their necks are often partially occluded by the spine apparatus, a structural complex of uncertain nature. The spine might therefore be a kind of calcium "trap" in which cation levels could rise far beyond those found in main dendritic processes with their mitochondrial buffers and greater opportunities for diffusion. Conversely, the calcium levels needed for triggering calpain are in excess of those needed for many cellular events—it will be recalled that neurons filled with the calcium chelator EGTA exhibited normal excitatory postsynaptic potentials. Together these features provide for a triggering event that would not occur during each physiological event but instead would be restricted to unusual circumstances. Something of this sort would seem to be needed if the memory mechanism were not to modify synapses during every synaptic transmission.

(c) *The mechanism produces effects that are likely to be very long-lasting.* Nearly all cytoplasmic chemistries (e.g., phosphorylation and methylation) are designed to produce rapid and fully reversible effects; proteolysis is virtually unique in that its consequences are irreversible. A priori, then, we can expect even a reasonably brief period of calpain activation to produce effects that will persist for long, and perhaps very long, periods. The hypothetical mechanism satisfies the all-important requirement of accounting for the extreme duration of memory.

(d) *The consequences of activating the mechanism are known to occur after physiological stimulation and are likely to be of functional importance.* The calpain mechanism was discovered while searching for a process that could elicit the types of biochemical and structural changes that correlated with long-term potentiation of synaptic transmission. We have shown that calpain mimics the persistent increase in glutamate binding sites found in LTP and, at least in one model system, causes morphological reorganization as well. It is not known whether similar effects actually occur during learning, but the very fact that they are triggered by physiological stimulation greatly increases their plausibility as memory substrates.

(e) *It is possible that activation of the mechanism requires contemporaneous events in several spines.* This point is better considered after a discussion of the types of circuitries within which memory storage is likely to occur.

Before discussing attempts to test this hypothesis, it is appropriate to list those features of it that require more convincing documentation. The localization of calpain and its substrates to the synaptic region is based solely on subcellular fractionation experiments, and these are prone to several types of error. We are currently using immunocytochemical techniques to determine whether the enzyme and fodrin are actually found in dendritic spines. We also lack a direct demonstration that the calpain mechanism is triggered by physiological events. While technically difficult, it should be possible to test this prediction of the model. If these experiments are successful, then the likelihood that the proposed mechanism is actually involved in synaptic plasticity will be greatly increased; in some senses, it is difficult to imagine that the activation of a protease with the consequences produced by calpain does not result in lasting changes in function.

D  *Behavioral Tests of the Hypothesis: Evidence That Different Types of Memory Involve Different Chemistries*

A number of behavioral predictions follow from the hypothesis, the most prominent of which are that memory should be accompanied by an increase in glutamate receptors and that inhibition of calpain should produce amnesia. To test the first of these, we carried out a collaborative study with Richard Thompson, who had shown that eyelid conditioning in the rabbit causes changes in neuronal activity and synaptic strength in the hippocampus (Berger and Thompson, 1978, 1982; McCormick et al., 1982). Removal of the hippocampus does not affect conditioning in this task, so the observed physiological modifications are presumably related to some aspect of behavior not sampled in Thompson's experiments. In any event, we measured the number of binding sites in conditioned rabbits, animals given random pairing of the CS and UCS (a procedure that does *not* affect hippocampal physiology), and naive rabbits. The trained rabbits showed a 30% increase in glutamate receptors compared with the other groups (Mamounas et al., 1984).

To study the behavioral effects of drugs that block calpain, we used osmotic minipumps filled with various concentrations of leupeptin and connected to intraventricular cannulae. These pumps operate continuously for 14 days and slowly infuse the drug into the cerebrospinal fluid, in this way producing a substantial inhibition of calpain (and other thiol proteases) throughout the brain.

In collaboration with Dr. Ursula Staubli, we first tested the effects of various concentrations of leupeptin on feeding, drinking, body temperature, and spontaneous activity as measured by line crossings and rearing. At the highest concentrations (20 mg/ml; estimated CSF concentrations of 50–100 $\mu$M), leupeptin had little or no effect on feeding and drinking, but did appear to influence the spontaneous activity of some but not all rats. Lower drug levels (8 mg/ml) had no detectable effect on activity. A variety of behavioral tests involving a memory component were used, perhaps the most informative of which was the 8-arm radial maze. In this, the rat is presented with 8 alleys radiating from a central platform with a reward at the end of each alley. After several days of testing, the animal acquires an optimal strategy of entering each arm but once, thereby avoiding arms in which the reward had already been consumed; on some tests the rats were removed from the maze after the fourth choice and then returned 10 min to 4 hr later. Leupeptin caused a very significant impairment in this task, particularly on those trials in which delays were used; control animals infused with saline or aprotonin, an inhibitor of serine proteases, behaved as well as normal rats. Leupeptin was effective even at concentrations only one-half those that did not produce any measurable change in two tests of spontaneous activity or on feeding and drinking (Staubli, Baudry, and Lynch, 1984).

The rats were well trained on the maze before infusion of the drugs was started, and it was evident that established memories were unaffected; thus the animals rapidly entered the alley arms and consumed the rewards found there, behaviors never seen in naive rats. Moreover, the errors they committed did not fall into any obvious pattern (e.g., perseveration); nor did the animals appear slower in racing from one arm to the next.

Very different results were obtained when shock avoidance learning was used. In one experiment rats were placed in a well-lit chamber adjacent to a dark chamber and, when they entered the latter, given a mild foot shock (passive avoidance). Twenty-four hours later both leupeptin-treated and control animals remained in the illuminated compartment. In active avoidance, the rats learned to escape from one compartment to the next in a 10-sec interval before a foot shock was applied; again leupeptin-treated animals mastered this test and were similar if not identical to controls 24 hr later (Staubli, Faraday, and Lynch, 1985). These experiments allow us to add pain thresholds to the list of physiological/psychological variables unaffected by leupeptin—this is particularly interesting since drugs that block peptidases, enzymes that degrade neuropeptides, have been reported to elevate tolerance to pain markedly in rats (de la Baume et al., 1983).

Intuitively, the radial maze seems to be a complex form of learning requiring the rat to remember a large amount of information on each day's testing in comparison with that needed for successful performance of shock avoidance. It is also exquisitely sensitive to even small lesions in forebrain structures (and in particular the hippocampus), and this is probably not true for shock avoidance. This caused us to look for a task mediated by the telencephalon that involved memory of a very few, specific cues. As will be discussed at length later, the olfactory system is for the most part restricted to the telencephalon, and smell learning requires the same structures needed for the 8-arm maze. Accordingly, we trained rats on successive 2-odor discriminations and, when they had become expert at this, applied leupeptin.

The drug produced a profound impairment in the acquisition of correct responses to novel odor pairs and thus blocks even seemingly simple memory tests that are mediated by telencephalic connections (Staubli, Baudry, and Lynch, 1985).

The above results suggest that the selective action of leupeptin on learning cannot be explained by side effects of the drug that are differentially manifested over a gradient of complexity. An obvious alternative explanation is that the neural substrates of avoidance conditioning versus olfactory and spatial memory utilize different chemical processes. If this were to be so, then we might expect to find that treatments that disrupt the former would have lesser effects on the latter. Protein synthesis inhibitors are known to produce profound impairments of avoidance conditioning (e.g., Squire and Barondes, 1974; Flood et al., 1978), although there is some controversy as to the mechanism by which they exert this effect (Gold and Sternberg, 1978). Accordingly, we established treatment regimens with a synthesis inhibitor that severely disrupted memory as measured in shock-conditioning tests and then tested for their effects on olfactory learning. We could find no evidence for impairment in either the acquisition or retention of 2-odor discrimination learning (Staubli, Faraday, and Lynch, 1985).

These results are most encouraging, but further work using other treatments that manipulate calpain are badly needed. Unfortunately, a very limited pharmacology is available, and the characterization of the chemical and behavioral effects of available inhibitors has only just begun. Further work along these lines, combined with studies using new inhibitors now being developed in several laboratories, should allow a more rigorous test of calpain's involvement in memory storage.

However, it seems unlikely that behavioral pharmacology can be used satisfactorily to test hypotheses about memory. Drugs produce unwanted effects, and controlling for these is a difficult and seemingly endless task. Memory is a higher-order phenomenon dependent upon the normal operation of physiological processes that can be influenced by experimental manipulations intended for the putative memory mechanism. Testing of the hypothesis described here will require the development of systems in which it is possible to monitor the flow of information through circuitries and the identification of how this is changed so as to produce memory. Synaptic plasticity needed for memory can be found in brain circuitries—finding out whether it is actually used will require that we identify where and when the changes that lead to memory occur.

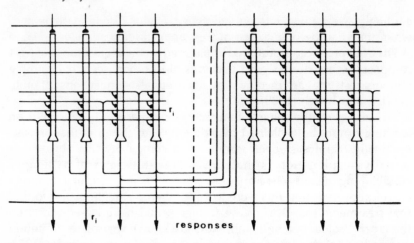

Figure 4
A model of an associative network as designed by Kohonen, Lehtio, and Oja. Note that the system is laminar, involving iterative connections both from outside the two subsystems and from within, as provided by internally generated associative projections (from Kohonen et al. in Hinton and Anderson, eds., *Parallel Models of Associative Memory*, 1981, p. 111).

## II Combinatorial Systems

Having shown that cellular chemistries exist that would allow synapses to serve as storage elements for memories of indeterminant durations, we can now take up the question of the types of circuitries that might use these processes in storage and retrieval. A salient feature of the memory system is its enormous capacity for forming associations between elements selected virtually at random from an unlimited array of possibilities (for a discussion of capacity, see Standing, 1973), a point that has been recognized since Aristotle (Anderson and Hinton, 1981, p. 15). This has led many theorists to assume that memories are represented in a distributed form, presumably in the cortex, and that the representations are densely interconnected (for reviews, see Willshaw, Buneman, and Longuet-Higgins, 1969; Kohonen, Oja, and Lehtiö, 1981; Cooper, Lieberman, and Oja, 1979; Palm, 1982; Habeles, 1982), possibly in a random fashion (Feldman, 1981). This requires circuitries that have a strong combinatorial property in which axonal projections from scattered cells interact in the dendritic fields of a collection of neurons that have no defined spatial relationship to each other. Figure 4 provides an example. This of course raises the question of whether the cerebral cortex and related structures actually possess such organizations, and if so, to what degree. In a later section, I shall summarize neuro-anatomical data showing that circuits that fit this description are found in at least some parts of the mammalian cortex. But are such arrangements a common characteristic of cortical organization, as presumably is required if they are to mediate cognitive events? Anatomical and physiological studies over the past two decades have vastly increased our understanding of cortical organization, but for the most part these have not been concerned with developing "macromodels." There is, however, older comparative literature that points to some generalized statements, and in this section I shall briefly discuss two of these and argue from them that combinatorial circuitries are probably represented throughout the mammalian telencephalon.

## A   Circuit Design and Dendritic Allometry

Many of the cellular constituents of the mammalian brain are highly correlated with absolute brain size. Dendritic length (Bok, 1959) and the packing density of neurons in the cerebral cortex (Sharif, 1953; Bok, 1959; Tower and Young, 1973) can be predicted from brain size by power equations with exponents of about $+1/3$ and $-1/3$, respectively ("the cube root rule"). Thus the increase in the number of neurons does not keep pace with increases in absolute brain size across mammals, but the dendrites grow ever longer. This results in an enormous difference in the amount of dendritic (and presumably axonal) arborization that must be supported by the neuronal cell body as one proceeds from mouse to man.

Why has the mammal linked the size of neuronal arborizations to absolute brain size with all of the biochemical and biophysical changes that this must entail? A number of authors have made the suggestion that increased dendritic area permits greater interaction (Jerison, 1973), something that would be required if additional inputs were added to a pool of combinatorial neurons. This point is illustrated in figure 5. Two patterns of connectivity known to occur in the brain are illustrated, one of which requires dendritic expansion to accommodate added input, and a second that does not. Panel A shows a case in which axons from one region disperse their terminals throughout much or all of a second brain area so that any one input neuron makes only a small number of contacts with any particular target neuron. In panel B, the input neurons focus their terminal fields so that a cell-to-cell arrangement is created. It is most unlikely that an individual synapse can bring a cell to firing threshold, and therefore in panel A near-simultaneous activity in more than one input axon is needed to cause a discharge of a cell in the target array—thus responses in the second brain area require a combination of events in the first region. This organization will be referred to as a *combinatorial array*. In B, concentration of synapses from one axon on a single target means that activity in one cell in the

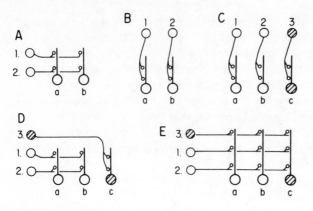

Figure 5
Two patterns of connectivity are illustrated. In (A), the inputs (1 and 2) provide one contact for each of the two target cells, while in (B), the two inputs are segregated so that "1" provides two synapses for "a" and "2" generates two contacts for "b". The arrangement in (A) will be called combinatorial and that in (B) topographic. Additional input ("3") to the topographical organization can be accommodated by simply adding a third neuron to the target field ("c") without any changes in the already present inputs and targets (panel (C)). This will not work for the combinatorial network as illustrated in (D) if the already present mode of operation is to be maintained; that is, the new input will disrupt the combinatorial character of the circuitry. In (E), the combinatorial character of the circuitry is retained in the face of new input. This requires the addition of new neurons to the target field but also the expansion of dendritic trees and axonal arborizations.

first brain region can activate a sufficient number of synapses on the target to cause it to discharge. With these arrangements any organization found in the first array will be preserved in the second, and the system is thus punctate and *topographic*.

A new cell ("3") is added to an expanded topographic first array in panel C. To maintain the organization already present, it is necessary simply to add a third neuron ("c") to the second array. As shown in panel D, this solution does not work for the combinatorial system, since the added cell in the first array does not gain access to the representation of that array in the second brain region. In order for the operating system to be maintained, it is necessary for the added cell to form contacts with the neurons already present in the second region, and therefore the extension of the dendrites of those neurons (panel E). Thus expansion of combinatorial but not topographic organizations requires expansion of axonal and dendritic arborizations.

Combinatorial designs produce a situation in which discrete stimulation of inputs causes a widespread and scattered excitation of the target, while topography results in strictly localized responses. Both schemes are probably found throughout the vertebrates, and it is likely that they form a continuous dimension rather than distinct categories, but the cube root rule suggests that the combinatorial pattern has been carried to great lengths in the mammalian forebrain.

## B  Emergence of the Mammalian Telencephalon from a Combinatorial Reptilian Pallium

Comparative studies have often proved useful in deciphering basic patterns in exceedingly complex biological systems such as the mammalian cortex, since it is sometimes possible to identify organizational and functional features in simpler systems that have become obscured in more evolved (homologous) variants. It is generally agreed that the mammalian cortex and hippocampus evolved from a much simpler reptilian pallium, suggesting that the latter may be useful in identifying general features of circuitry that are very probably still present in the former.

Reptiles and birds have forebrains dominated by a dorsal ventricular ridge (d.v.r.), a massive structure protruding into the lateral ventricle from the lateral wall of the hemisphere. This is not found in any living group of amphibians—in fact, modern amphibians typically have a modest expansion of the medial dorsal wall of the telencephalon, the pallial zone thought of as a primordial hippocampus. Since all extant birds and reptiles possess a d.v.r., it can be assumed that this feature was present in their last common ancestor; to conclude otherwise would require that we accept the unlikely idea that virtually the same structure evolved independently several times. Mammals clearly do not possess a d.v.r., and therefore it is not likely that their last common ancestor (perhaps 200 million years ago—mya) had one either. The fossil record indicates that the separation of the lineage that led to the mammals occurred very early in reptilian evolution (325 mya) and that the divergence of the lines that produced the modern reptiles happened shortly after the appearance of the stem reptiles. Combining these points, we arrive at a scenario in which the earliest reptiles gave rise to a group(s) that contained a primitive version of the d.v.r. and a group(s) that did not; the former led to the birds and reptiles, the latter to the mammallike reptiles (the therapsids) and ultimately the mammals.

The subclasses of mammals (marsupials, monotremes, and placentals) have brains markedly different from those of reptiles/birds in that the telencephalon contains a very large cortex and an extremely laminated, stereotyped hippocampus. The three groups of mammals have long and separate evolutionary histories, suggesting that the cortex and hippocampus first appeared in something like their current forms with the earliest mammals. There is little evidence in the fossil record to indicate that the expansion of the brain needed to accommodate the cortex occurred in the ancestors of the primitive mammals; thus the Mesozoic therapsid reptiles had tubular and relatively small telencephalons not unlike those of the amphibians (Hopson, 1979; Quiroga, 1979). This suggests that some aspect of the transition from the mammallike reptile to the mammal grade triggered the radical reorganization of the telencephalon required for the cortex and hippocampus to emerge in their present forms. With this background, we can now take up the argument that the mammalian telencephalon is dominated by combinatorial arrangements in the context of the evolutionary histories just described.

While modern reptiles have brains greatly evolved from the ancestral condition, they nonetheless contain the best clues to the organization of the brains that gave rise to those of three classes of terrestrial vertebrates. Figure 6 summarizes some recent hodological work on the lizard pallium. The primitive cortex (pallium) of the lizard clearly incorporates a combinatorial element. The neurons in the medial pallial wall are collected into a dense cell body layer that gives rise to a homogeneous dendritic field. This zone is innervated by the lateral cortex. Even small lesions in the lateral area cause axonal and terminal degeneration extending across the entire array of medial pallial dendrites; moreover, there is evidence for an extensive anterior-posterior spread of projections (Ulinski, 1976). This matches the description of an iterative combinatorial array and shows a strong resemblance to the circuit model illustrated in figure 4. The medial pallium projects to the dorso-medial and dorsal cortices and repeats the pattern of axons running through a sequence of dendrites; this also appears to be true for the commissural inputs from the contralateral hemisphere (Lohman and Mentink, 1972; Lohman and Van Woerden-Verkley, 1976). It is very likely that the cortex contains topographically organized inputs from the thalamus (Northcutt, 1981), but the intracortical anatomy clearly has an iterative character to it.

If this cortical organization resembles that of the earliest reptiles, then it follows that much of the mammalian telencephalon emerged from a structure that already possessed a strong iterative combinatorial element in its design. Reptiles and especially birds have evolved the d.v.r. system, which appears to have punctate, topographic organization in which increases in size must be accomplished primarily by adding neurons.

C   *Circuit Designs and the Mechanisms of Memory*
The arguments made in the preceding two sections can be summarized as follows:

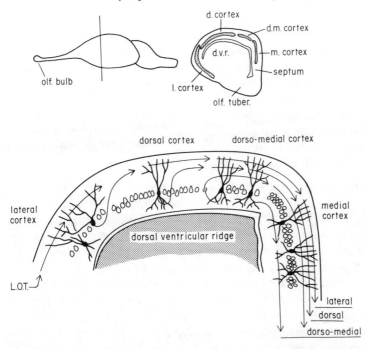

Figure 6
Schematic illustrating aspects of the intrinsic organization of of the reptilian pallium.
The frontal sections are approximately at the plane shown in the small drawing to the
top left. The pallium overlays the lateral ventricle and the subjacent dorsal ventricular
ridge (d.v.r.); going from lateral to medial, it includes the lateral, dorsal, dorso-medial,
and medial cortices (l.cortex, d.cortex, d.m.cortex, and m.cortex in the drawing to the
top right). These cortical zones consist of a packed cell body layer and cell-sparse apical
and basal dendritic layers. The lateral olfactory tract terminates in the outermost portions
of the apical dendrites of the lateral cortex, which in turn sends monosynaptic projections
to the top of the apical dendritic field of the medial cortex and possibly to that position
in the intervening cortical areas as well. Fibers from the dorsal cortex appear to end in
a lamina immediately below that occupied by the inputs from the lateral cortex in the
dorso-medial and medial cortices. Dorso-medial cortex projects to the apical and basal
dendrites of the ipsi- and contralateral medial cortex as well as to the contralateral dorso-
medial cortex. (Possible ipsilateral associational systems have not been investigated.) The
medial cortex provides a massive input to each of the three cortical fields lateral to it
(not illustrated). It is important to note that the projections from a given frontal plane
spread across a wide extent of the anterior-posterior portion of the entire pallium. (Based
on work by Ulinski and several other authors; see text.)

(1) Increases in the number of neurons in mammalian cortex result in neurons with longer, more elaborate dendrites. This suggests that added input is to some important degree integrated into the dendritic fields of cortical neurons and by implication that these cells are designed to respond to combinations of synaptic contacts from many different afferents.

(2) The evolutionary precursor of the mammalian hippocampus and cortex was very probably organized as an iterative, combinatorial system; accordingly it is likely that the mammalian structures retain this basic design feature.

These points, combined with the fact that at least some cortical neurons have widely ramified axonal fields, make it likely that combinatorial circuitries are well represented in the cerebral cortex. As will be argued later, neuroanatomical experiments provide direct evidence that the hippocampus, which has been related to memory processing, is also organized as an iterative combinatorial system.

Combinatorial and topographic circuit organizations can be seen to place different constraints on the sites and possibly mechanisms of memory storage. In combinatorial systems, a very large number of potential interactions from widely spaced inputs can occur on the dendrites of an individual cell; widespread changes in a target cell produced by physiological events in a few afferents would result in perturbations in all other sets of potential combinations on that cell. Accordingly, it would seem necessary to restrict modifications to those synapses that act together (i.e., as a combination) to initiate the change. This raises the question of how synapses located on disparate parts of the dendritic tree of a neuron might through simultaneous or near-simultaneous action produce changes in their own strength without disturbing intervening contacts. One possibility is suggested by the recent hypothesis that dendritic spines contain voltage sensitive calcium channels (Perkel and Perkel, 1985); if this were correct, then we could imagine that depolarizations (elicited by transmitter release) in separate spines electronically summate and thereby cross a threshold for opening calcium gates (see Shepherd, this volume), and activating the biochemical processes discussed earlier. Spines located between the two depolarized units would also experience a drop in membrane potential, but this would not necessarily be of a magnitude sufficient for affecting their voltage sensitive calcium channels. Computer models of spines and dendrites should provide some indication of the feasibility of this triggering mechanism. Topographic systems may not face this problem. For example, in an extreme point-to-point system, the output of one cell would be restricted to the dendritic field of a single target neuron;

under these circumstances whole cell changes in the target would be equivalent to modifications of the individual synapses formed with the unitary input.

Topographic and combinatorial systems also face different problems with regard to the maintenance of memory. In the latter, the breakdown and replacement (turnover) of spines and synapses would presumably result in the loss of the representations of experience encoded as modifications of those synapses (for a discussion of turnover and stability, see Lynch, Larson, and Baudry, 1985). If memory is stored as a neuron-wide modification in topographic projections, then there would be no necessary reason for it to disappear in the face of continual and even rapid turnover of synapses.

## III The Olfactory System as a Model for Studying Combinatorial Circuitries

We can now ask what types of processing are likely to be carried out by combinatorial circuitries with plastic synapses. And, directly pertinent to the theme of this review, how we can study their role in different types of memory.

Both questions require some type of model system that incorporates the generalized features proposed above, and yet is sufficiently simple that it can be used for neurobiological investigations. An adequate test system would also need intimate and well-defined connections with subcortical structures thought to be involved in memory processing. In the following sections, I shall argue that the olfactory projections into the telencephalon meet these requirements and can be used to study memory as it is found in "higher" mammals, including man.

The discussion has three parts. First, the anatomy of the olfactory bulb projections into the pyriform cortex will be reviewed and the argument made that these form an excellent example of a combinatorial system. Second, additional anatomical data will be used to show that two of the second-order olfactory structures are regions thought to be vital to the encoding of some types of memory. Third, some recent results showing that lesions of the hippocampal formation produce deficits in the rat's olfactory memory will be discussed and the point made that these closely resemble the amnesia syndrome found in humans with temporal lobe damage.

### A The Anatomy of the Olfactory Cortex Is Combinatorial

The primary receptors for touch, vision, and hearing are topographically projected upon their first-order relays in the central nervous system in such a way that adjacent regions of the sensory epithelium innervate adjacent groups of neurons in the target nuclei. Olfaction exhibits a degree of topography, but it lacks the precision found in the other modalities; a single odor excites a particular portion of the bulb, but distinct odors have overlapping target zones (Pinching and Doving, 1974; Stewart, Kaver, and Shepherd, 1979; Jourdan et al., 1980; Jourdan, 1982; Lancet et al., 1982). In the projections of the first-order relays, the differences between the olfactory system and other modalities become still more obvious. The topography in initial organization found in vision, hearing, and touch is maintained through subsequent stages of their central projections, while the imperfect mapping in the olfactory bulb is lost altogether or at the least greatly obscured in its first-order projections. Thus each area of the bulb projects to all regions of the pyriform cortex (Price, 1973; Broadwell, 1975; Skeen and Hall, 1977) and all areas of the pyriform receive inputs from many segments in the bulb (Haberly and Price, 1977; Schwob and Price, 1978).

Studies using retrograde transport of two labels have convincingly shown that individual mitral cells have axons with branches in widely separated regions of the pyriform cortex (Luskin and Price, 1983a). While some type of broad topography may yet be found in the bulbar projection (See Scott, McBridge, and Schneider, 1980), the collected body of neuroanatomical data leaves little question that the system is an excellent example of a combinatorial organization.

The trajectories and terminal fields of the lateral olfactory tract (L.O.T.) axons are extremely laminated (Haberly and Price, 1977; Skeen and Hall, 1977; Shammah-Lagnado and Nefrao, 1981; Carlsen, De Olmos, and Heimer, 1982). The pyriform and entorhinal cortices are bounded on their outer surfaces by a cell free molecular zone (layer I) composed of the dendrites arising from a tightly packed layer (layer II) of modified stellate neurons. The olfactory tract and its collateral branches travel at the very top of the molecular layer and generate a dense terminal field that innervates its outer one-half (layer Ia) (for a review see Broadwell, 1975; Heimer, 1978). This produces an iterative arrangement in which a given fiber provides more or less the same synaptic input to successive elements in a very long array of similar dendrites, i.e., iterative combinatorial design of the type illustrated earlier (figure 5).

The secondary stages of the olfactory system repeat the pattern laid down by the bulbar efferents. Only some of the features of this can be illustrated here. The modified stellate cells innervated by the L.O.T. generate a massive associational system that ramifies throughout the pyriform cortex as well as spilling over into the entorhinal and frontal cortices (Haberly and Shepherd, 1973; Price, 1973; Krettek and Price, 1977b; Haberly and Price, 1978a,b; Luskin and Price, 1983a). While association fibers spread diffusely over primary and secondary olfactory

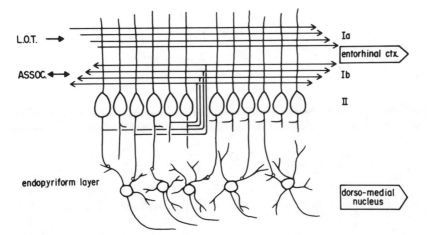

Figure 7
Schematic of the organization of the pyriform cortex. The drawing, following largely
from the work of Price and colleagues (see references), summarizes some of the major
features of the pyriform circuitry. The lateral olfactory tract (L.O.T.) enters an array of
dendrites and forms an extensive terminal field in layer Ia. The dendrites belong to a
layer of neurons whose cell bodies form layer II and whose axons collateralize in layer
Ib, as a dense associational (assoc.) projection, and send branches into the endopyriform
nucleus (i.e., the deep layer of the pyriform cortex).

cortex, they terminate with great precision in the inner part of the
molecular layer (layer Ib) immediately subjacent to the terminal field
of the L.O.T. (Luskin and Price, 1983b). In all likelihood, this system
represents a second iterative, combinatorial arrangement superimposed
on that formed by the output of the olfactory bulb (figure 7).

The layer II stellate cell axons also have branches that end in the
deep layers of the pyriform that constitute the so-called endopyriform
nucleus. This "nucleus" extends along much of the anterior-posterior
extent of the pyriform and sends fibers to the dorso-medial nucleus of
the thalamus (Price and Slotnick, 1983). It can properly be considered
the output stage of pyriform circuitry.

B    *The Olfactory Cortex Is Directly Connected to Memory-Related
Structures*
Beyond the pyriform cortex, the olfactory system diverges into two
great projections, one through the hippocampus and the other into the
dorso-medial nucleus and frontal cortex. There is considerable evidence
that these higher-order stations are vital to memory processing in humans; their roles in olfactory memory will be considered in a later
section (for physiological studies see Yokota, Reeves, and MacLean,

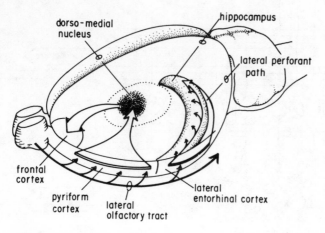

Figure 8A

Illustration of two olfactory pathways through the telencephalon. The olfactory bulbs (at the front of the brain) generate the massive lateral olfactory tract, which innervates the contiguous pyriform and entorhinal cortices. The first of these projects into the dorso-medial nucleus of the thalamus, a structure that in turn innervates the frontal cortex. The entorhinal cortex produces the perforant pathway, the major afferent of the hippocampal formation.

1970; Tanabe, Iino, and Takagi, 1975; Tanabe et al., 1975; Wilson and Steward, 1978, Habets, Lopes da Silva, and Mollevanger, 1980; Yarita et al., 1980).

The hippocampal wing of the system consists of a series of stages: olfactory bulb and pyriform, superficial layers of the entorhinal cortex, dentate gyrus, regio inferior ($CA_3$), regio superior ($CA_1$), subiculum, and deep layers of the entorhinal cortex (figures 8A and 8B). The pyriform and entorhinal cortices are structurally quite similar, both containing a superficial layer of stellate cells and a deep layer of projection neurons. However, while the superficial layer of pyriform cortex projects directly to the deep layers, those in entorhinal cortex enter into the hippocampus, which then ultimately innervates the deep layers. In some senses, the hippocampus forms a long loop interposed between the superficial and deep layers of the entorhinal cortex, a point which is emphasized in figures 8A and 8B.

The successive stages of the olfactory-entorhinal-hippocampal sequence of arrays repeat many of the features described for the superficial layers of the pyriform cortex. The stellate cells of the lateral entorhinal cortex (which in most respects is a posterior continuation of the pyriform) form a compact layer II and with outwardly ramifying dendrites that

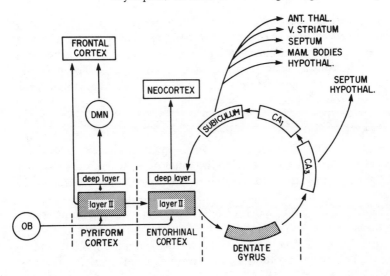

Figure 8B
Schematic summary of two olfactory pathways through the telencephalon. Note that according to this reconstruction, the hippocampus serves to relay olfactory information to several subcortical regions but also acts as an intermediary between superficial and deep layers of entorhinal cortex. The similarity between the layer II cells of olfactory cortex and the granule cells of dentate gyrus is suggested by the shading used in the drawing.

constitute a molecular layer (layer I). The L.O.T. axons travel across the surface of the cortex and sequentially innervate the outer portions of the molecular layer (layer Ia; Kosel, Van Hoesen, and West, 1981), with the inner zone (layer Ib) receiving associational fibers from the pyriform cortex as well as the entorhinal cortex itself (Beckstead, 1978; Haberly and Price, 1978a,b). There is every reason to assume that those projections form iterative combinatorial arrangements.

The entorhinal stellate neurons of layer II generate the massive lateral perforant path that enters the hippocampus (see Hjorth-Simonsen and Jeune, 1972; Steward and Scoville, 1976; Schwartz and Coleman, 1981) and deposits terminal fields in the dentate gyrus and regio superior (see, e.g., Blackstad, 1956; Hjorth-Simonsen, 1971; Steward, 1976; Matthews, Cotman, and Lynch, 1976a,b). Discrete areas of the lateral entorhinal cortex project very broadly to the dentate gyrus (Wyss, 1981) in a manner somewhat reminiscent of the olfactory bulb projections to the pyriform cortex.

The dentate gyrus, the primary target of the lateral perforant path, bears a number of resemblances to the stellate cell layer of the pyriform and entorhinal cortices. It is composed of densely staining neurons that form a packed cell body layer with a broad dendritic molecular layer. Branches of the diffusely organized lateral perforant path travel across the outer one-third of the molecular layer, establishing successive contacts with hundreds, if not thousands, of granule cells. The perforant path-dentate gyrus connection thus constitutes a combinatorial array, not unlike the L.O.T.-entorhinal system.

The mossy fiber axons of the granule cells have collateral contacts with a group of adjacent polymorph neurons whose axons generate a dentate gyrus commissural/associational system; the axons and terminals of this system are located in the inner one-third of the molecular layer (i.e., in a position comparable to the layer Ib zone occupied by the pyriform-entorhinal commissural/associational system; Zimmer, 1970; McWilliams and Lynch, 1978). The associational-commissural projections spread over much of the dentate gyrus, with individual fibers coursing sequentially through long arrays of granule cell dendrites, in essence forming a second iterative, combinatorial array (for a review, see Lynch, Rose, and Gall, 1978).

The output of the dentate gyrus is restricted to a collection of large pyramidal cells that constitute the regio inferior ($CA_3$) of the hippocampus proper. This is an iterative connection in that individual mossy fibers contact a long array of pyramidal cells. However, the projection is discrete in that narrow longitudinal segments of the dentate gyrus restrict their efferents to equivalently narrow segments of the regio inferior (Blackstad et al., 1970; Lynch et al., 1973).

The regio inferior generates a massive commissural/associational network that covers the regio inferior itself as well as extending into the neighboring regio superior ($CA_1$—Laurberg and Sorenson, 1981). This system repeats the now-familiar theme of axons passing across a sequence of parallel dendrites making contacts within a well-defined lamina proximal to a packed cell body layer. It also exhibits considerable spread along the longitudinal axis of the hippocampus (Swanson, Wyss, and Cowan, 1978) and can be categorized as iterative combinatorial. The regio superior is unique in the sequence of stages in that it does not generate its own associational system but instead projects simply to the subiculum and deep layers of the entorhinal cortex (Hjorth-Simonsen, 1971). These deeper zones also appear to receive direct input from the regio inferior.

The subiculum and deep layers of the entorhinal cortex can be considered as the output elements of the hippocampal formation; the subiculum projects back to the regio superior (Berger et al., 1980) and to entorhinal cortex (Sorensen and Shipley, 1979), ventral forebrain, anterior thalamus, and mammillary bodies, while entorhinal cortex sends axons to the temporal neocortex (Kosel, Van Hoesen, and Rosene, 1982;

Rosene and Van Hoesen, 1977), amygdala (Aggleton, Burton, and Passingham, 1980), and prefrontal cortex (Swanson, 1981). It should also be noted that the regio inferior sends axons outside the system into the septum and basal forebrain (Raisman, Cowan, and Powell, 1965; Swanson and Cowan, 1977).

As is evident, there are a number of similarities in the organization of the five successive stages of circuitry from the olfactory bulbs through the hippocampus, the most salient of which are summarized in figure 9. Note that associational systems occupy a large part of the dendritic fields of each stage and represent the dominant connections in the pyramidal cell fields. In fact, there appears to be a general shift in the balance of extrinsic input versus associational connections as one proceeds from the pyriform to the regio superior. The granule cells, while sharing some of the features of the layer II stellates, exhibit some unusual characteristics, including an indirect associational system and a peculiarly restricted projection field (which incidentally generates one of the most unusual terminals in the brain).

The general similarity of the organization found in the chain just described with that of the lizard pallium should also be noted.

The anatomy of the second great branch of olfactory projections through the forebrain, that to the dorso-medial nucleus of the thalamus and the frontal cortex, is organized somewhat differently than the pattern just described for the path through the hippocampus. The target cells of the olfactory bulb in the pyriform cortex project to the endopyriform nucleus (Price and Slotnick, 1983), an extended layer of neurons lying adjacent to the external capsule along much of the anterior-posterior extent of the telencephalon, and this region sends numerous axons to the dorso-medial nucleus (Krettek and Price, 1977a, and references therein). Discrete injections of horseradish peroxidase into the DMN lead to the retrograde labeling of neurons along much of the length of the endopyriform nucleus, indicating that the inputs from this area overlap extensively (Price and Slotnick, 1983).

The dorso-medial nucleus fibers terminate in layers I and III of the sulcal frontal cortex (Krettek and Price, 1977a). To the extent that DMN efferents travel tangentially throughout layer I, the system can be viewed as an iterative combinatorial array. Further discussion of the system would require information on the projections of the cells whose dendrites extend into layer I. It seems likely that both vertical and horizontal interactions occur, that is, that some axons from upper layers of the frontal cortex converge on cells in the deeper layers, while others extend parallel to the surface, innervating successive pyramidal neurons. If so, then the cortex would afford a sequence of arrays as in the hippocampus, but substituting layers of cells for the spatial segregation of input ele-

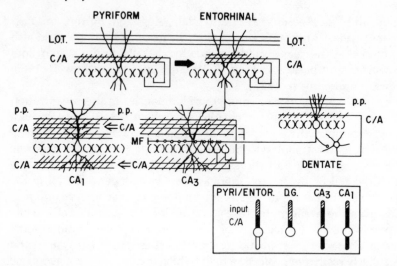

Figure 9
Some points of similarity and difference between the successive stages of the olfactory-
hippocampal pathway. Pyriform and entorhinal cortices form one unit; note that the
pyriform associational system makes contact with the commissural/associational (C/A)
target region of entorhinal dendrites. The dentate gyrus neurons bear a number of similarities to those in the pyriform/entorhinal, but there are several major differences. In
the dentate, the commissural/associational projections are generated by a sparse population
of polymorph cells rather than by the granule neurons themselves. Moreover, the granule
cells vastly outnumber the polymorph neurons; presumably, then, the dentate gyrus
associational system must have operating features that are greatly different than those
of the other steps in the sequence. Note also that mossy fiber axons that constitute the
output of the dentate gyrus are tightly compressed in a narrow proximal zone of CA$_3$
pyramidal cell dendrites and form giant boutons; these arrangements are very unlike
the other connections in the olfactory-hippocampal system.

Field CA$_3$ is composed of giant pyramidal cells but respects the general arrangement
of a commissural-associational zone in the inner dendritic field and a distant dendritic
layer for extrinsic inputs. The mossy fibers disrupt the similarity by occupying very
elaborate spines in the initial dendritic shafts. The CA$_3$ neurons also use their basal
dendrites as a C/A region. The CA$_3$ commissural/associational projections continue into
CA$_1$, where they form the dominant afferent. CA$_1$ is the only step in the circuitry that
does not generate a commissural-associational feedback system.

The insert summarizes the lamination of the various stages in the olfactory-hippocampal
system, and emphasizes the variations in amount of dendritic arborization used by each
stage for commissural-associational afferents (p.p.: perforant path).

ments and their targets. It should be noted that the pyriform associational system extends into layer I of the same frontal areas innervated by the dorso-medial nucleus—this strongly suggests that primary and tertiary pyriform projections interact in this neocortex.

Thus the olfactory connections in the higher levels of the forebrain possess both iterative and simple combinatorial patterns; in the case of the hippocampus, the similarities to the lower levels of the olfactory systems are so pronounced as to suggest comparable processing modes. The thalamic element of the system seems to represent a shift from an iterative to a simple combinatorial mode of operation, while the cortex may offer some of the same interactions as the hippocampus.

A further and possibly critical difference in the DMN and the hippocampus targets of the olfactory projections is that the latter almost certainly contains many more cells than the former. Thus we can assume that individual cells in the DMN receive inputs from pyriform cells representing different odors; the dentate gyrus-hippocampal system conversely may contain enough cells to generate distinct cell populations for a vast number of olfactory cues.

C   The Hippocampus, Dorso-Medial Nucleus, and Olfactory Memory

The evidence summarized above leaves little doubt that the sequential stages of the brain's olfactory processing system provide a well-defined example of combinatorial circuitry of a type that, from allometric and comparative analyses, we expect to find running throughout the cortex and possibly other regions of the forebrain. Moreover, we have added much anatomical detail that might well be present in the cortex (though presumably obscured) and, in any event, should be helpful in developing ideas about the operation of combinatorial circuitries in memory. Finally, the intimate relationship between olfaction and two brain structures critical for memory in humans (the dorso-medial nucleus and hippocampus) briefly mentioned in earlier sections has now been illustrated in some detail. This brings us to the third argument for using olfaction and olfactory anatomy as a model system for studying memory in combinatorial circuitries, namely, that lesions in the hippocampus and dorso-medial nucleus in laboratory animals produce memory deficits for smells that resemble some amnestic conditions in humans.

Early studies (Allen, 1941) showed that ablation of the hippocampus had little effect on olfactory behaviors, a result that contributed to the toppling of the idea that the hippocampus was the cortical representation of smell. Recent work, however, indicates that the DMN, frontal cortex, and hippocampus do make major contributions to olfaction in laboratory animals and possibly in humans as well. Slotnick and coworkers (Slotnick and Katz, 1974; Nigrosh, Slotnick, and Nevin, 1975) have shown that rats learn successive olfactory discriminations in a manner quite different from that for auditory or visual problems. Specifically, the animals require a large number of trials to solve the first problem, but with successive odor discriminations they acquire each new correct response in only a very few trials. Similar effects are obtained using successive reversals. But in the same testing apparatus, the animals do not show anything like rapid learning of visual or auditory reversals, even after dozens of problems. Slotnick hypothesizes that rats acquire learning sets for olfactory cues in much the way that primates do in solving a series of visual and auditory problems. That is, he argues that the rat first learns something about the task itself (rather than any particular odor used in the problem) and then uses this information in subsequent problems to learn rapidly and remember the correct odor. Animals with lesions in the dorso-medial nucleus do not acquire the olfactory learning sets and behave more or less as normals do on successive auditory and visual discriminations (Slotnick and Kaneko, 1981). In these experiments, it was found that large lesions of the posterior pyriform cortex and lateral olfactory tract did not interfere with the acquisition and use of learning sets and specific olfactory information. Since the lesions undoubtedly severed the connections between the olfactory bulbs and the entorhinal cortex, it can be assumed that the hippocampus made no contribution to olfactory behavior in Slotnick's paradigm.

Ursula Staubli and I have recently reexamined the possible role of the hippocampus in olfactory behavior using a somewhat different paradigm. In this the rats are trained to choose alleys in a maze (for water reward) on the basis of odors. The position of the odors is randomized from trial to trial so that the task has no spatial component to it. Each day a new pair (or triad) of odors is used and intertrial intervals (during which the animals are locked in the last selected goal box or removed to their home cages) are varied from 1 to 10 min. The rats exhibit more or less the same pattern of learning described by Slotnick in his bar-pressing experiments in that many errors are made on the first 2 or 3 odor pairs, but ultimately the rats learn to choose correctly in only 3 to 5 trials. Lesions of the entorhinal cortex have no detectable effect on this task when the intertrial intervals are kept below 3 min, but produce profound impairments on those days in which longer delays are used. Thus the hippocampus is not required for the sensory, motivational, or even attentional aspects of the problem, but it does seem to play a role when the rat must store information for more than a few minutes. As a further test of this, we trained rats on a short delay problem for 10 trials, then waited an hour, and retested the rats with the same odors but with their significance reversed. Normal or control lesion animals would continue to respond to the previously correct odor, while the entorhinal-lesioned animals immediately acquired the correct (formerly incorrect) odor. Thus in these animals even a well-learned odor had no effect on subsequent performances only 1 hr later (Staubli, Ivy, and Lynch, 1985).

There are a number of parallels between these results and the deficits found in humans with temporal lobe lesions or dysfunction. The rats in our experiments clearly recalled their prelesion experience in the olfactory maze, since they were able to use the learning set in those odor problems involving brief intervals. Persons with temporal lobe damage are known to have access to memories formed well in advance of their injury (for a recent review, see Squire, Cohen, and Nadel, 1985). The anterograde amnesia experienced by these patients is not complete, and in particular they are able to learn puzzles that require considerable practice even by normals (for a recent review, see Cohen and Squire, 1980; Squire, 1982); from Slotnick's results we can infer that the hippocampus is not needed for rats to acquire learning sets that require extensive training on the first few trials.

Thus, as predicted from its anatomical relationships, the hippocampus does participate in higher-order olfactory functions, though, at least in the rat, not in the sensation or discrimination of smells. While a great deal more work needs to be done, at this time it appears to be part of the circuitry used by the animal to store information about particular odors.

It has been recently reported that the hippocampal patient H.M. has a severe impairment in olfactory discrimination (Eichenbaum et al., 1983); persons suffering from Korsakoff's disease, which is thought to involve damage to midline brain structures including the DMN, are known to have elevated thresholds for smell (Jones, Moskowitz, and Butters, 1975), as are patients with prefrontal damage (Potter and Butters, 1980). The extent of the brain damage suffered by these patients is unclear, but the results clearly point to a connection between higher-order olfactory structures and the systems used by the human brain to learn complex material.

## IV Synaptic Plasticity, Combinatorial Connections, and Memory

Having identified a specific brain system organized along lines expected for a "cognitive" memory system, we can now ask how it might process information and what the previously described synaptic plasticity adds to this.

A   *Representation or "Naming" of Stimuli*

As described, it is known from studies using the deoxyglucose method that a single odorant excites a reasonably discrete patch of cells in the olfactory bulb and that different patches are associated with different smells. We also know that axons from discrete regions of the bulb distribute themselves widely and quasi-randomly across the olfactory cortex. It is very likely that multiple inputs are required to cause an individual pyriform or entorhinal neuron to discharge; this is certainly the case throughout the hippocampus, which, as we have seen, is organized along lines similar to those of the pyriform/entorhinal cortices. Accordingly, one stimulus will lead to the firing of individual stellate neurons scattered across the entire extent of olfactory cortex. It would seem that nothing has been gained and indeed much lost by this transformation, since one mode of stimulus identification (spatial location) has been sacrificed. Why?

Presumably, in nature, many odors (like cues in the other sensory modalities) are composed of several elements. But, unlike the other senses, the olfactory system must deal with a world in which few, if any, rules govern what can and cannot be combined into a unique stimulus associated with a constant object. In a word, the olfactory environment lacks predictability. It has been suggested that the development of connections in other sensory pathways reflects (and exploits) those features of the environment that, across the evolution of the species, occurred in a reliable (predictable) pattern (Greenough, 1984). Spatial contiguity in the visual system provides an example— adjacent elements that move together in visual space can be assumed to be aspects of a single stimulus, whereas elements that occur at disparate locations and/or move separately can be assumed to be different objects. Topographic organization of the first stages of sensory processing is appropriate for capturing this information. Similar spatial rules are lacking for olfaction, and rigid topographic representations would preclude the association of elements that constitute the signature of a single object in the environment. In fact, even the earliest stages of the brain's olfactory system must possess the capacity to combine into a unique output virtually any collection of events from an extremely large set of possibilities that can occur at the first steps of sensory processing. In essence, then, the quasi-random combinatorial organization of the olfactory system reflects the character of the information that it processes.

The above arguments lead to the idea that complex stimuli should provide a means of analyzing the operation of the combinatorial circuitries under discussion. Consider the case illustrated in figure 10, in which an odor with two components (A and B) is used. Two patches

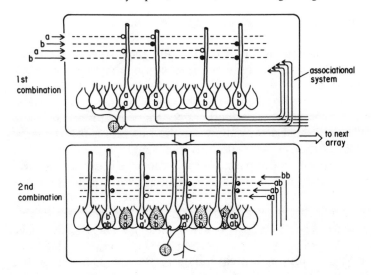

Figure 10
Combinatorial operations of circuits of the type found in pyriform cortex. The assumption
is made that two or more afferents must be simultaneously active to cause a target cell
to discharge and that axons form contacts more or less at random. Four cells jointly
innervated by two of the afferents are illustrated in the top panel. Some of the combinations
involve inputs from the same source (i.e., "a" inputs, synapses noted by open circles,
or "b" inputs, synapses indicated by filled circles), while others are innervated by mixtures
of "a" and "b". When the neurons respond to the inputs (aa; bb; ab; ba) they send
impulses that activate inhibitory interneurons and prevent further discharges; impulses
are also sent along the collaterals that form the associational system, and second-order
combinations occur on the cells these axons jointly innervate. This results in further
mixing of the "a" and "b" input signals and the emergence of a cell population that
responds only if both "a" and "b" are given together.

on the bulb are activated containing cells labeled "a" and "b", respectively. The axons from the two olfactory regions will jointly innervate cells scattered randomly throughout the pyriform cortex; this
will result in neurons activated by one of three combinations (aa, ab,
bb). Thus one set of units unique to the composite stimulus is produced.
The remaining two sets would be identical to those occurring whenever
A or B was present as a single stimulus.

The associational system offers the opportunity for a second combinatorial operation involving (aa), (ab), (bb) stellate cell outputs. Given
the quasi-random nature of the system, a given cell is twice as likely
to connect with an element unlike itself as it is with one like itself;
thus of the nine equally likely combinations only one involves the
mixture of (aa) with (aa). Probabilistically then the large majority of

second-order combinations require both "a" and "b" bulbar cells to be activated.

Additional combinations should occur as the system enters and passes through the hippocampus. These provide two valuable functions. First, the percentage of cells responding to A or B alone will be decreased still further, reducing the chances that the complex AB will be mistaken for either of its components or another odor that contains one of them. Second, the additional arrays allow for the processing of ever more complex odors. When an ABC stimulus is presented, activating patches "a", "b", "c" on the bulb, partial combinations (e.g., *ab*, *bc*, *ac*) will appear in the pyriform-entorhinal cortex along with smaller numbers of *aa*, *bb*, and *cc* cells. A second combinatorial operation will produce a majority of cells that require all three stimulus elements, but a sizable number responsive to only two will remain (e.g., *ab*, *bb*). Successive combinations rapidly reduce this percentage, leaving a population of neurons that fire only upon presentation of all three elements in the composite stimulus. Thus, the larger the number of odors to be combined, the more useful are sequential combinatorial arrays.

The hippocampus emerges from this analysis as a higher-order structure that utilizes its sequential combinatorial arrays to complete the job, begun at lower levels of the olfactory chain, of forming unique representations of complex environmental cues. In a very real sense, it is simply a continuation of a processing chain that can be traced back to the olfactory bulbs. However, "macroanatomy" tells us that there is more to the story. The pyriform cortex, entorhinal cortex, hippocampus, etc., are independently connected to different brainstem, thalamic, and telencephalic areas. Thus, successive links in the chain of connections leading away from the bulb not only provide for sequential processing, but also serve to integrate the olfactory signal with diverse nonolfactory brain regions. It is also likely that the type of processing will change with changes in the internal anatomy of the different stages (see section III.B) in the olfactory hippocampal system.

The bulbar-pyriform connection probably contains equivalent input (mitral cells) and target (modified stellate cells) arrays, and the stellate cells have relatively short dendrites. Moreover, the input from the bulb occupies no more than 50% of the dendrite. If we assume $10^6$ mitral and stellate cells and a total of $10^4$ synapses on each of the stellate cell's dendrites, then a given mitral cell can only contact a small number of stellate cells. Note also that an input may form more than one contact with a particular target, reducing still further the size of the population of neurons it contacts; this means that the number of stellate neurons jointly innervated by two particular input axons is very low ($<<10^4$). Whenever the size of the input and target arrays is large relative to the size of the receptive surface of individual target elements, a "sparse" matrix will be formed, and this appears to be the case for the bulbar pyriform and the pyriform feedback associational systems. For this system to generate a combinatorial representation, it is necessary that a large number of elements in the input array be activated, as indeed appears to be the case for olfaction (see above). If several thousands of mitral neurons discharge to a single "primary" odor, then the low connectivity index of the pyriform system is overcome and a substantial population of jointly innervated neurons will appear. An arrangement such as this limits the number of "primary" odors, but maximizes the differences in the populations activated by these or any combinations of them.

The dentate gyrus contains hundreds of thousands of cells with relatively short dendritic trees; the entorhinal projections to these presumably generate a sparse combinatorial matrix. The commissural-associational system is poorly developed and involves a relatively small group of polymorph neurons. This suggests that further combinations do not occur within the dentate itself. Moreover, the granule cell axons are topographically organized along the length of the hippocampus and occupy a very narrow lamina along the cell bodies of the pyramidal neurons; each of the $CA_3$ cells cannot receive more than a few hundred terminals from the entire dentate gyrus. This suggests that the representations in the dentate gyrus do not form many combinations on individual pyramidal cells. However, each granule cell axon forms a massive bouton, which makes several synaptic contacts with its $CA_3$ target. It appears, then, that the granule cells are well suited to transmit faithfully (i.e., without further combinations) the combinations formed in their dendrite to individual $CA_3$ cells. What functions might such a system perform? The response of the dentate gyrus to the perforant path varies across behavioral states (Winson and Abzug, 1978) and many subcortical and brainstem regions send projections into a narrow zone immediately beneath the granule cells (the infragranular layer), where they presumably interact with interneurons and polymorph cells that provide facilitatory and inhibitory input to the granule neurons. Possibly, then, these extrinsic inputs use the dentate gyrus as a gate for controlling the flow of information from the entorhinal cortex to the hippocampus (Winson and Abzug, 1978, have made a similar proposal).

The pyramidal cells are morphological units quite unlike the small cells that occupy the stages that precede the hippocampus proper. They have much longer and elaborate dendritic trees and thus much larger synaptic populations than granule or stellate cells. Moreover, as mentioned, the great majority of the dendrite is taken up with associational connections. It is possible that the size of the synaptic population begins to approach the size of this input array, thereby creating a situation in which a given associational fiber might contact a significant percentage of its potential targets. The system would thus form a much "denser" array than is found in the pyriform-entorhinal or dentate gyrus stages. This would be useful if only a small number of $CA_3$ cells were activated by the granule cells responding to the presentation of a complex stimulus; a dense matrix formed by the $CA_3$ associational system with $CA_3$ dendrites might then serve to generate a combinatorial representation that utilized a larger population of $CA_3$ cells than that excited by the mossy fibers. The switch from sparse to dense arrays may thus be necessary when the "size" of representations to be combined is small. (This discussion proceeds from a simplifying assumption that roughly the same number of synapses are needed to cause a target cell to discharge. At all stages of the circuitry this threshold value influences the actual "sparseness" of a network and the size of its representations.) Other possible images of dense arrays are discussed in a later section.

Finally, it was noted that the field $CA_1$ has no associational feedback and possesses a topographic relationship to the subiculum. Thus the final combinations in the system probably occur in the dendrites of $CA_1$, where $CA_3$ fibers mix while $CA_1$ itself projects the final representation without further modifications.

Several features of olfactory anatomy were not incorporated into the above analyses, including possible interactions between patches of cells in the olfactory bulb and feedback inhibition in the bulb and each of the processing stages discussed. There is no evidence that any of these exhibit topography, and, to the contrary, what is known of local recurrent (inhibitory) interneurons suggests that they are diffuse in their projection patterns (see drawings in Cajal, 1911; Lorento de Nó, 1934). Systems of these kinds can be expected to "sharpen" neural messages by suppressing firing in neighboring cells and perhaps to place limits on the number of output elements active at any given moment. This latter property could prove useful in a combinatorial system that is open to a very large array of potential inputs.

## B  *Recognition Memory*
The representational function proposed above does not require synaptic plasticity. However, there are reliability problems inherent in the system, and modifications of synaptic strength could serve to "stabilize" representations. In the following discussion, I shall assume that long-term changes will occur in the synapses on target cells that are jointly innervated by a small group of afferents when those afferents fire together at high frequency.

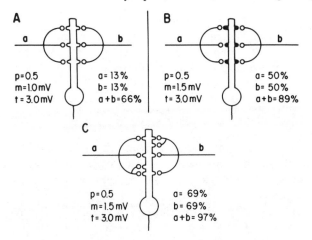

**A**

a — b

p=0.5
m=1.0mV
t=3.0mV

a= 13%
b= 13%
a+b=66%

**B**

a — b

p=0.5
m=1.5mV
t=3.0mV

a= 50%
b= 50%
a+b=89%

**C**

a — b

p=0.5
m=1.5mV
t=3.0mV

a= 69%
b= 69%
a+b= 97%

Figure 11
Effects of long-term potentiation on the reliability of representations in combinatorial systems. In panel (A), two axons ("a" and "b") converge on a target cell, each forming three synapses. It is assumed that the probability of release for any terminal is 1/2 and that each release event produces a 1.0 mV (EPSP); the threshold for discharging the neuron is set as 3.0 mV. Thus, the cell will fire only 13% of the times when "a" or "b" fires alone (i.e., on those rare occasions when all three of the axon's terminals release their transmitter). When "a" and "b" fire together, the probability of three release events occurring (and the target firing) rises to 66%. The induction of long-term potentiation (panel (B)) results (according to this hypothesis) in an increase in the size of the unit EPSP to 1.5 mV, a change that, as illustrated, markedly increases the likelihood that the target cell will react to the simultaneous occurrence of "a" and "b". Thus a more reliable representation is constructed. In panel (C), the effects of adding new contacts between the axons and the dendrite are illustrated. Assuming that the system is potentiated, this produces a situation in which *either* input has a reasonable chance of firing the neuron.

It follows from the anatomical properties described earlier that the number of contacts between any two cells in an iterative combinatorial network will be small; since transmitter release is probabilistic, a degree, and perhaps a high degree, of failure is inherent in the system (i.e., the postsynaptic cell does not respond to its inputs). Accordingly, for any group of axons there will be a scattered population of jointly innervated target cells, a variable subpopulation of which will discharge on any given activation of the inputs. The system might well interpret the same cue differently on different encounters.

Synaptic plasticity could serve to increase the reliability of the representations generated by a combinatorial organization. Consider the case illustrated in figure 11A, in which a neuron is innervated by two axons (a and b), each of which generates three synapses; the probability of release is set at 0.5 for all boutons, and the unit response (for one release event) is 1.0 mV. The firing threshold for the cell is placed at 3.0 mV, and thus the neuron responds to three or more (but not fewer) release events. With these paramaters the cell responds ("spikes") to stimulation of one axon alone about 13% of the time and on 66% of the occasions in which both axons are activated. If all cells jointly innervated by a and b were to follow these rules, there would be a considerable variation in which of these cells detect the combination over successive presentations.

Increases in the size of the unit response from 1.0 to 1.5 mV (figure 11B) by the potentiation mechanisms discussed earlier will have a major impact on this situation, since release from any two terminals would now suffice to drive the target. Probabilistically, this could be expected to occur on about 90% of the trials for a sequence of trials in which both axons are stimulated, a clear improvement in reliability.

If the potentiation effect is large enough, then a population of cells that reliably fire to the stimulus will emerge, a development that should be passed through the successive combinatorial arrays, producing an even more distinct and reliable representation of the cue at each of the levels of the olfactory chain.

As discussed, the potentiation effect is cumulative and is accompanied by structural/chemical changes in existing contacts as well as the addition of new synapses. These effects, and in particular synaptogenesis, would eventually produce a situation in which either input alone could drive the target with some reliability (see figure 11C). Thus we might imagine that with repeated exposure, the system moves through a sequence in which a target neuron fires with greater and greater reliability to simultaneous activity in the two inputs and eventually reaches the point at which it discharges to either alone. The recipient cell would then become an "or" rather than an "and" unit in that it would respond to either of the two inputs typically used in combination to discharge it. When applied to a single-component stimulus, this becomes a variant of the process already described that leads to an increase in the size and fidelity of the neural representation of the cue. For compound inputs, reducing the combinatorial requirements has additional effects, and in particular produces a situation in which higher-order cells might respond even when a normally necessary element of the stimulus complex was missing. Under these circumstances, plasticity could be used to allow recognition of a complex stimulus from one of its fragments, a property that might be of considerable value in dealing with odors that vary slightly in their composition and yet must be reliably identified by the animal.

Considered in this light, some aspects of olfaction should resemble recognition memory in humans. In particular, the link between assembling a reliable representation (or pattern) for the cue and the occurrence of memory has been well documented for visual recognition memory; subjects thus recognize previously seen visual stimuli that were perceived as faces but rapidly forget comparable cues that are seen as unrelated elements (Freedman and Haber, 1974). Similarly, collections of letters that can be assembled into words, even very novel words, are remembered far better than collections that cannot. Note also that parts of well-learned visual cues can be perceived or recognized as the whole, a feature that again would be expected from the analysis given above. While the analysis of visual recognition memory will be greatly complicated by the topographic stages of processing that precede the postulated combinatorial networks, it should nonetheless be possible to attempt some comparisons between it and olfactory memory in laboratory animals. This point will be discussed in a later section.

A key idea in the above analysis is that high-frequency activity produces synaptic change. But what causes the high-frequency activity? Hippocampal pyramidal neurons exhibit high-frequency bursting when depolarized; however, typical EPSPs do not elicit this because of the extremely potent feedback (e.g., Andersen, Eccles, and Loyning, 1964; Kandel, Spencer, and Brinley, 1961) and feedforward (Lynch et al., 1981; Alger and Nicoll, 1982) inhibition generated by the interneurons found at every level in the structure. Neuroanatomical studies (Mosko, Lynch, and Cotman, 1973; Rose and Schubert, 1977) indicate that at least some of these interneurons are innervated by afferents originating in the septum and brain stem. I have elsewhere suggested the possibility that these "minority" inputs serve to regulate interneuron activity, and hence the likelihood that firing bursts will be elicited by active synapses in the hippocampus (Lynch, Rose, and Gall, 1978). According to this idea, events that occur during active searching and/or that are unexpected, conditions thought to activate brainstem and septal afferents, would serve to alter the balance of interneuron activity and thus open the way to high-frequency activity and plasticity (figure 12).

C  *Higher-Order Association*
According to the arguments of the previous section, adding plasticity to the combinatorial circuitry that comprises the olfactory system makes for more reliable representations of odors; memory thus emerges as an aid to perception. Even such apparently simple sensory operations as treating multiple elements as a single cue or recognition of a compound stimulus from a subset of its constituents were postulated to be experienced-based processes.

However, memory is usually taken to involve not only recognition but a particular kind of association between elements, namely, a cor-

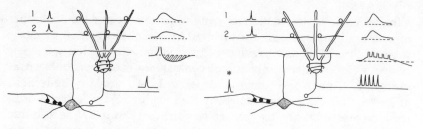

Figure 12
Generation of high-frequency outputs by combinatorial cells. A cell innervated by two excitatory inputs ("1" and "2") and a feedback inhibitory interneuron (dark cell) is illustrated. Under normal conditions, two inputs produce EPSPs, which sum and cause the cell the discharge; the recurrent collateral activates the interneuron, which then produces a large IPSP in the target, blocking further spiking. On the right side, the two inputs arrive at the same time as an inhibitory input, which blocks the interneuron; the summed EPSPs from the excitatory inputs now produce a prolonged depolarization in the target cell body, resulting in high-frequency bursting.

relational relationship between sensory elements or motor acts that does not alter the perceptual records that go into the association. This section will advance the argument that the processes described earlier can, with some additions, be used to accommodate one class of associational memories.

Let us consider the case in which an olfactory signal becomes associated with a visual one. This requires the integration of olfactory and visual representations of an environmental event, an operation for which the hippocampus is ideally situated. Auditory and visual information reaches the pyramidal cell fields (see below)—how it gets there is unclear, but neuroanatomical experiments indicate that cat and primate cerebral cortices contain a series of connections leading from sensory fields to the entorhinal cortex. The entorhinal cortex has medial and lateral subdivisions, both of which project into the dentate gyrus and hippocampus (Hjorth-Simonsen and Jeune, 1972). The olfactory projections are restricted to the lateral entorhinal area, while the extrinsic afferents of the medial zone, and particularly those of the stellate cell layer that generates the output to the hippocampus, are something of a mystery (Van Hoesen, Pandya, and Butters, 1972; Beckstead, 1978). In any event, we do not know whether olfactory and nonolfactory information are segregated within the entorhinal cortex, but for purposes of simplicity I shall assume that this is the case and that the nonolfactory pathways pass through the medial region. This will produce a situation in which cells responsive to complex visual stimuli and odors are found throughout the hippocampus. The fragment recognition process described above could provide a mechanism for associating these. Suppose two such specified cells are driven by their inputs (i.e., both environ-mental cues are present) during a period of reduced inhibition and therefore fire together at high frequency. Long-term potentiation would occur at the synapses of the two neurons on the cells they jointly innervate, thereby producing a target that responds to either input alone (an "or" cell). Presumably the above process would pass through the same sequence postulated for recognition to fragment recognition of odors; initially, a reliable representation of the association forms in response to repeated exposure to the two cues, and then either cue gains the ability to trigger the entire representation by itself.

As mentioned, memory associations are usually thought to leave intact the perceptions of elements that have been combined. In the hypothesis under discussion, this would require that the combinations that form the association occur at a stage in the succession of combi-natorial arrays *after* a complete representation of the elements has been formed and projected out of the chain. In the case of the olfactory circuitry, we might imagine that complete representations of even com-plex odors are achieved by the olfactory bulb and pyriform cortex. The replicas of olfactory cues found in the final stages of intrahippocampal connections could then be combined with nonolfactory inputs without disturbing the representation of odors.

It should be noted that the arrangement of olfactory connections proposed in preceding sections makes no provision for associations *between* olfactory cues, since the near-simultaneous arrival of two odors will result in a single representation beginning at the earliest stages of processing in the brain. When two well-learned odors are used, the system presumably will retain its earlier representations and form a new one composed of parts of each as well as an equivalent set of combined elements. Behavior then might vacillate depending upon the relative balance of odors on any given presentation or inhalation.

## D  Recall
The crossing of two chains with combinatorial links produces phys-iological association, but does not provide us with a psychological association in the sense of input A triggering the representation of in-put B. To the contrary, the combinatorial events occurring in the higher-order array would produce a representation of A plus B that would have little in common with those formed in that array by A or B alone; in essence, it would be a pattern of activity triggered by either of the inputs, but with connections and associations unique to itself. It might thus be analogous to a concept such as "cheese," which is presumably

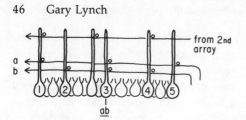

Figure 13
Schematic representation of the problems associated with "recalling" representations in combinatorial arrays. Two associational feedback axons ("a" and "b") are shown traveling through an array of dendrites forming contacts in a random fashion; a sizable number of neurons (1, 2, 4, and 5) receive inputs from one or the other of these fibers, while a much smaller group of cells are jointly innervated (#3 in the figure). These combinatorial cells form the representation of the input ab. A fiber from a higher array that enters the network is far more likely to synapse with a target neuron connected with either a or b but not both than it is with one in the smaller population of dually innervated cells. Accordingly, conjoint activation of the "recall" signal with the signal ab will lead to discharges in neurons that are not part of the ab representation ("1" and "4" in the figure).

constructed from representations for an odor and a visual object, but which has associations that are unshared by any of those elements.

Association between the two input stimuli in the hierarchical system under discussion would have to be mediated by feedback to each from the higher-order array. (It is possible that the representations "a" and "b" communicate directly with each other; this is better discussed after considering the hierarchical case.) This would provide for a type of recall to the network. The major problem with this is simply how the feedback-recall signal could become associated with spatially dispersed neurons, and only those neurons, that form the representation that entered into the association. This problem is illustrated in figure 13, in which a single feedback fiber enters the representation array and interacts with two axons from the external signal. Note that these two fibers jointly innervate one cell (which is thus part of the representation), but also *singly* innervate other cells (which therefore are unresponsive, and hence not part of the representation). As is evident, the feedback-recall axon is far more likely to contact one or more cells that are singly innervated than it is to contact the much smaller number of jointly innervated neurons. Using the rules described earlier, we find the high-frequency activity in the signal (a and b) and the feedback will most likely result in potentiation of cells that are not part of the representational ab. Not only does the feedback-recall signal fail to activate the constituent of the higher association, but it also creates confusion of the ab representation by producing b and a cells.

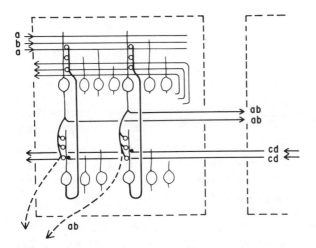

Figure 14
Possible solution to the problems of developing selective associations between representations in combinatorial arrays. Two ab combinatorial cells are formed using inputs and associational feedback as described in the text. The primary array generates vertical and spatially restricted projections to a second layer of neurons, which project back in a discrete topographic fashion to the first layer; thus a vertical positive feedback loop is created and patterns in the second layer are replicas of the combinatorial representation in the first layer. A signal from a second array (cd) enters the second layer and forms synapses at random, some of which are on the replicas of the combinatorial ab neurons. If the ab and cd neurons generate high-frequency firing bursts at about the same time, long-term potentiation will occur in those synapses of the cd projections that innervate second layer ab neurons. Subsequent presentation of cd alone will then trigger these cells which in turn will activate some fraction of the ab neurons in the primary (first layer) array, resulting in a situation in which activation of cd produces a partial activation of the representation for ab.

Some of these problems are obviated by using a *replica* of the representation as shown in figure 14. In this, columns vertical to the combinatorial array are used—each cell in the combinatorial array projects to a second-layer neuron and the output of the second-layer neurons form very potent synapses on the same neurons that innervate them (i.e., positive feedback). Finally, we hypothesize that the feedback-recall axons innervate the second-layer cells rather than those in the representational array.

The figure illustrates how this type of circuitry can be used as a crude recall device. Under these conditions, cooperativity between the feedback-recall synapses (from the higher-order array ab/cd) and those from the primary array (ab) occurs on the dendrites of individual replica neurons, thereby producing long-term potentiation. If repeated several times, this would lead to a situation in which the recall input alone would trigger the replica cell to activate a cell in the primary representation.

We might think of this as a case in which the representation for an odor triggers that for the concept of "cheese," which activates a lower array for a visual object. This purely hypothetical "replica" system would require two features: (1) the absence of an associational-feedback system and (2) a high degree of connectivity between the recall axons and the dendrites of the "replica" cells (i.e., a relatively "dense" matrix). Feedback would combine the outputs of the cells and activate neurons that were not part of the representations to be recalled. A dense matrix would be needed if the "recall" signal were to locate the replica neurons driven by a particular representation. Thus we would expect these cells to have dendritic fields large enough so that an individual neuron samples a high percentage of the total axonal ("recall") input provided by the higher-order representation. Despite this, we must assume that the recall signal connects with only a fraction of the "replica" cells and hence provides for partial activation of the primary representation.

Other solutions to the problem of recall from combinatorial networks become possible if we modify the rules for long-term potentiation. Consider, for example, the situation illustrated in figure 15. In this, combinatorial operations of the type already discussed involving input fibers and associational feedback are carried out in the apical dendrites, while the basal dendritic field is reserved for associative recall inputs from cells in other arrays. This places the recall elements outside the zones where representations are formed and stored, but still leaves the problem of connecting the recall axons with the very small percentage of cells that participate in a given representation. A possible solution to this would be to make synaptic change contingent upon activity in the target cells; in this way potentiation of synapses would occur only on those cells (i.e., that representation) active when the recall signal arrived. On subsequent occasions, projections from the second representation (e.g., *ab/cd*) would trigger only those cells in the primary array with which it had at some time been temporally associated.

What events in the postsynaptic cell might serve to assist in modifying the strength of the recall synapses? A simple and effective rule would be to make plasticity contingent upon cell spiking in the time period during or immediately preceding the arrival of the recall signal; thus we might imagine that the activation of a particular representation (i.e., discharges in a dispersed cell population) by its inputs *transiently* affects those cells in such a way that a subsequent recall signal could be connected with them. This is a somewhat modified form of a synaptic change rule proposed by Hebb (1949) in which temporal association of an excitatory input and the spiking it causes strengthens the input,

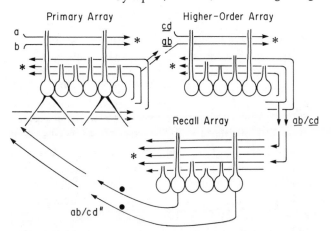

Figure 15
A second possible recall circuit. In this, two representations (<u>ab</u> and <u>cd</u>) in primary arrays are combined in a higher-order array to form the representation <u>ab</u>/<u>cd</u>. Collateral branches from the associational feedback system of this higher array then enter a third collection of neurons and develop a second version of the signal <u>ab</u>/<u>cd</u> there. This set of neurons is postulated not to use associative feedback and LTP to develop additional combinatorial operations; moreover, its axons are assumed *not* to discharge at a frequency or with a pattern sufficient to generate LTP by themselves on target dendrites. The output of the third array ("recall") projects back to the cell groups that form the primary representation, where they form a very dense matrix with the basal dendrites; activation of the recall signal in combination with the primary inputs (a and b) results in potentiation of the recall synapses on those cells innervated by the a and b and by the associational neurons they activate (i.e., on those cells that form the representation <u>ab</u>). Asterisks denote axon collections that can produce LTP by cooperative action on target dendrites, while the solid circles mark projections that potentiate only when combined with other inputs.

an idea that has proved useful in computer simulations of neuronal networks (see Cooper, Leiberman, and Oja, 1979, for an example). Here we use it in a different way in that spikes triggered by one afferent strengthen synapses activated shortly afterward by a second input; it should be emphasized, however, that there is no experimental evidence for the existence of a relationship between cell spiking and synaptic modification.

There are also aspects of long-term potentiation that could be used to link a dense input to specific postsynaptic cells. The cooperativity effect indicates that events in one group of synapses can facilitate modifications in a second (and vice versa). As discussed, simply coupling high-frequency activation in recall and input signals will produce LTP in the former on cells that do not participate in the representation elicited by the latter input. But suppose the recall signal is in some way too "weak" by itself to promote LTP; that is, we could imagine that a potent cooperative effect by the primary input on a target cell is a requirement for the recall afferents to strengthen their synapses. In such a case, the recall signal would potentiate only on those neurons that receive dense innervation from the primary input, which is to say those combinatorial cells that form the representation of the input. It is interesting in this regard that Levy and Steward (1976) and Kelso and Brown (1985) have shown that a population of afferents too small to potentiate when stimulated by themselves do so when coupled with much larger EPSPs from a second afferent. However, there remains the problem that recall afferents must be densely interconnected with their targets (again, the recall signal, in contrast with the primary input or associational feedback, must modify its connections with a specific and small population of randomly located neurons). Therefore, we must assume that many neurons in the target array will receive sufficient numbers of synapses from the recall input to promote cooperativity—solely in terms of numbers the recall elements cannot be a "weak" stimulus. Suppose, however, that the burst duration used by the recall fibers was insufficient to produce LTP. Under these conditions we could imagine that the recall would become potentiated only on those cells that received sufficient innervation from the primary input or associational feedback to elicit the cooperativity effect and LTP. Other variants of this hypothesis are possible. We have found that bursts of high-frequency stimulation too short to elicit LTP are effective in this regard when administered in a repetitive fashion (Staubli, Roman, and Lynch, 1985; Larson, Wong, and Lynch, in press). It is possible, then, that the recall input occurs in a pattern that is ineffective unless interwoven on a postsynaptic neuron with primary or associational inputs large enough to generate cooperativity.

To summarize, we can construct a recall device using the following postulates:

(1) the recall axons generate a dense matrix with the representational array;
(2) the recall elements utilize a physiological pattern that is of itself insufficient for LTP;
(3) when placed on cells receiving primary or associational synapses sufficient to generate LTP, the recall input is also potentiated.

These last two points can be tested experimentally using in vitro slices, and experiments designed for this purpose are in progress. But if these physiological requirements are satisfied, there will remain a final problem for this version of recall: the higher-order array was assumed to have associative feedback used to carry out iterative combinations with the production of LTP. Therefore, if these cells were to send recall fibers to the primary arrays, they presumably would produce LTP on a very sizable number of neurons independent of the presence or absence of other inputs to those neurons. Therefore, to make use of the device, we need to add a further complication, which is that the higher-order array projects to another array, which then densely innervates the primary arrays. This array would lack associative feedback and so would *not* combine the patterns it receives from the higher-order array; instead its cells would simply generate a second version of the combinatorial representations in the higher-order array. Therefore, it would not be necessary to assume that the "recall" array generates LTP-inducing patterns and so by itself might not potentiate its synapses in the primary array. This arrangement is illustrated in figure 15.

It will be noted that an asymmetry exists in both of the recall systems in such a way that lower-order representations can be connected with higher-order arrays with which they have no prior association. Thus the combination *ab/cd* (formed from the primary representations *ab* and *cd*) could send a recall signal while the representation *ef* was active; this would result in *ab/cd* synapses becoming potentiated on the representation for *ef* (or on replica cells for *ef*). Future activations of *ab/ cd* by *ab* or *cd* could thus stimulate the recall of *ef*. This creates the opportunity for serious confusion in which multiple representations are recalled simultaneously. This point will be considered below.

The recall devices might also be used to associate primary representations directly in different arrays. If the so-called replica cells actually exist in the cortex, then the neurons in a representation in one array could use their axon collaterals to stimulate cells indirectly in a second. Use of the second device, involving the pairing of representational input with a "weak" signal from a nonassociative "recall" array, could also be used to link parallel arrays. In this way a representation *ab* would form a second representation ab', which would then potentiate its connections in a primary array with cells receiving potent input. Such arrangements could be uni- or bidirectional and might underlie simple associations (e.g., "black-white").

Combining the two types of association (i.e., parallel and hierarchical) would have the advantage of sending two recall signals and thereby increasing the percentage of cells activated in the representation to be remembered. The addition of two types of recall (between primary representations and between higher-order and primary representations) may also dictate which representations are activated under a particular set of circumstances. Thus a higher-order array connected by feedback to many primary representations will have its greatest effects on those arrays that are also receiving recall input from other primary representations; environmental context will thus influence the flow of memory.

Other arrangements of these representational and recall elements could be designed. But it would seem more appropriate to consider the anatomical plausibility of the proposed devices. As discussed, it is likely that the pyramidal cell fields of the hippocampus are arranged as dense matrices in which a given neuron receives synapses from a significant percentage of the population of afferents; moreover, and most important, cells forming associational networks do in fact project to other groups that do *not* form associational systems of their own ($CA_3$ to $CA_1$). Thus, the hypothetical recall-associational circuits do not require anatomical elements other than those actually found in the hippocampus, and it is therefore not unreasonable to suggest that they are present in the cerebral cortex as well.

Further development and testing of the postulates discussed above require not only the identification of a particular set of neuronal cell types and circuitries but also a better description of the rules governing the plasticity produced by the interaction of different types of inputs. In particular, we need to use patterned stimulation in already potentiated and nonpotentiated inputs to determine if and how the former can facilitate the production of LTP in the latter. There has been surprisingly little work directed at testing rhythmic stimulation (i.e., short bursts given at different interburst intervals), but as mentioned we have found that very short bursts of activity do not elicit LTP unless given within certain patterns.

Table I summarizes representational and recall-association cells and networks that have been discussed. Note that two types of representational arrays are included, distinguished by the relationship of their dendritic length (and number of connections) to the size of the input array. Representations stored in arrays with short dendrites (e.g., pyriform-entorhinal cortices, dentate gyrus) are not likely to participate in recall networks, and indeed it does not appear that these receive major inputs other than their primary and associational afferents. When these project to large neurons (e.g., dentate gyrus to $CA_3$), then both representational and recall functions can be developed.

## E  Some Predictions from the Analysis

The above sections represent an attempt to depict how memory emerges from (or adds to) physiological operations in combinatorial circuitry as represented in the olfactory system, with additional speculation about the neocortex. According to this analysis, memory has its beginnings as an aid to stimulus representation, and is inextricably bound up in perceptual operations. This may not be true for odor *detection*. The

Table I

Properties of hypothetical representational and recall arrays

|  | Representation | Recall-Association |
|---|---|---|
| Inputs | Mixture of cues or mixture of primary representations | One representation from a primary or higher array |
| Circuit features | Sparse matrix when input is large[a] (e.g., bulbar-pyriform), dense matrix when input is small (? $CA_3$ - $CA_3$ associational system) | Output, and probably Inputs, form Dense matrices |
| Anatomical features | Inputs and associational feedback form laminated synaptic fields | Lacks Associational feedback (e.g., $CA_1$) |
| Physiological features | Sequential combinatorial operations (input followed by feedback)<br>Input, associational, and output axons can each produce LTP on target dendrites | Single Combinatorial operation by inputs—no feedback<br>Output fibers by themselves do not generate patterns that produce LTP—require a second input that by itself can cause LTP |
| Functions | Form a Unitary Representation of a complex input | Form a second version of a representation—link this with representations in other arrays |

[a]Size refers to the percentage of input fibers activated by a given cue or representation.

olfactory bulb has a convergent projection to a collection of nuclei along the base of the telencephalon, and these may be adequate for signaling the animal that an odor is present. But discrimination between countless numbers of stimuli (and thus "recognition" of a particular stimulus) presumably involves the expanses of the pyriform cortex with its combinatorial organization. Association, according to the model, is accomplished by representational-memory operations of the type seen in the pyriform but carried out in the higher-order arrays (the hippocampus) and involves combinations of olfactory and nonolfactory input. The following section deals with a few of the behavioral results that should be obtained if the various postulates are correct.

If odors are treated combinatorially, we should expect to find that a mixture of novel, equally intense odorants will be recognized by a rat as a single cue and, in fact, that this will be accomplished as easily as learning a single-element smell. This is counterintuitive and testable.

For example, after having learned to discriminate the novel complexes ABC and ABD from each other, rats would not be expected to recognize C versus D; that is, they should act as though C versus D is a new problem, since a fully combinatorial system will produce a representation of ABC that is nearly as different from the representations of its components as it is from those for any other single or multiple odor. Dr. U. Staubli has recently obtained preliminary evidence that fulfills this prediction. This may point to a fundamental difference between combinatorial and topographic systems; confronted with two novel complexes with redundant information (that is, information present in both complexes), topographic systems will quickly identify what is different, while the combinatorial system will not (again, assuming that all elements are of equivalent intensity).

The relationship between memory and representation also implies that prior experience will have a pronounced impact on the processing of current input. For example, consider the case in which the odor A has developed a defined representation in the olfactory chain through the hippocampus and the novel stimulus AB is then presented. In the previous discussion of complex stimuli it was emphasized that since all combinations are equally likely, AB will result in *ab* cells after two or three successive combinatorial operations. But if A has been previously experienced, all combinations are not equally likely and *aa* neurons will predominate from the earliest stages of processing. That is, many more cells innervated by two "a" axons will discharge than will cells jointly innervated by one "a" axon and one "b" axon or by two "b" inputs. In successive stages of iterative combination, many more cells innervated by *aa* will fire than will neurons receiving *ab* or *bb*. Thus the entire system will react to the complex stimulus as though it were the previously experienced element and, in essence, behave as a feature detector. (If we add recurrent inhibition to the network, this effect becomes more pronounced, since the weaker non-*aa* combinations will be more likely to be suppressed than the potentiated *aa* cells—i.e., masking.) If the stimulus AB is presented without previous exposure to either of its constituents, then the combinatorial system will proceed to generate a unique and reliable representation of it.

There is a now classic body of literature showing that experience early in development exerts profound influence on the perceptual operations of the adult visual system. To the extent the above analyses are correct, olfactory experience throughout adult life will influence future olfactory perception, and the system, being combinatorial, will have a difficult time detecting the presence of a weak novel element when it is added to a well-established olfactory signal. (Again, we are ignoring possible complexities added by events within the bulb.) One might not expect this from a purely topographic system. Familiarity with a "+" cue should not hinder, and might in fact help, the detection and recognition of a minor alteration (±). In any event, it should be possible to test for these deduced properties of olfaction in behavioral experiments.

Speculating further, we might also expect to find that any recall functions served by the hippocampus would be unidirectional. Since the hippocampus projects back into the neocortex via the deep layers of the retrohippocampal region (Kosel, Van Hoesen, and Rosene, 1982), it is possible that an olfactory input could activate a cortical representation. In this, the hippocampus is envisioned as serving as an association-feedback array of a type already described, but with the input (and feedback) target arrays in the cortex. An association between a cortical signal and an olfactory signal could then be constructed in the hippocampus and the cortical elements activated in subsequent episodes by the olfactory input alone. However, the hippocampus and entorhinal cortex do not project back into the pyriform cortex, and thus presentation of the nonolfactory signal would not result in activation of the earlier stages of olfactory processing. Thus, the nonolfactory cue would result in the appearance of only those portions of behavior associated with the odor cue that are triggered by the highest stages of olfactory processing.

The model also makes a number of specific physiological predictions. First, it suggests that many more cells in higher stages of the circuitry leading through the hippocampus will be more finely tuned to complex, specific odors than is the case at lower levels of the olfactory system. Second, the neurons that respond to a given stimulus will be spatially scattered and not restricted to a particular level of the pyriform/entorhinal cortex or the hippocampus. This follows from the assumption that the axons make synapses more or less at random as they travel through the array of target cell dendrites; therefore, inputs will converge on cells that have no particular spatial relationships. Moreover, since the entorhinal cortex, which provides the input to the hippocampus, is itself an iterative array for its afferents, we can assume that cells scattered along its dorsal-ventral extent will act combinatorially, and hence inputs will be generated to much of the septotemporal extent of the hippocampus. Third, the reliability of a cell's response to a stimulus (or the probability of finding a responsive cell) will increase with repeated exposures to the stimulus. Fourth, purely on anatomical grounds, it seems clear that the entorhinal cortex-hippocampus provides a set of arrays suitable for forming associations with nonolfactory stimuli, since it is at that level that equivalent amounts of the two forms of information first converge. This predicts that cells will be found in the hippocampus that respond when very specific olfactory and nonolfactory cues are given together and that eventually, with training, the same neurons will fire to either stimulus. The conclusion would also predict that lesions of the hippocampus should eliminate learned associations between specific olfactory and nonolfactory cues. I know of no data pertinent to either of these points, but they should be testable using laboratory animals. The idea that destruction of the hippocampus would cause the loss of memory material goes against the widely accepted conclusion that the hippocampus facilitates long-term memory storage but itself does not store memory. This conclusion comes mainly from work with brain-damaged people, and, although presumably true as a generalization, there remains the finding that hippocampal patient H.M. is unable to identify familiar objects on the basis of smell (Eichenbaum et al., 1983).

Unfortunately, there have been very few single-unit recording studies from the pyriform-entorhinal cortex or the hippocampus during the presentation of odors, but hippocampal data for other modalities are found in the literature. Many pyramidal cells (at least in the dorsal hippocampus, where nearly all recording studies have been conducted) respond to spatial cues; that is, they fire rapidly as the animal approaches or is placed in a given location. The cells are responsive to complex distant visual cues, as shown by O'Keefe and his associates (for a review, see O'Keefe, 1976; O'Keefe and Nadel, 1978). It should also be noted that hippocampal pyramidal cells have very low rates of firing and are often "silent" for long periods of time in rats moving freely through complex environments; this further emphasizes the point that these neurons are coded to very specific cues. The position of these spatial cells in the hippocampus has no detectable correspondence with the position of the environmental cues that trigger their activity or with one another; thus two adjacent neurons may discharge to completely different environmental cues located at opposite ends of the testing apparatus. It would indeed be remarkable if electrodes placed randomly in the hippocampus were to find the single neuron, among the hundreds of thousands of hippocampal cells, that is coded to a particular configuration of spatial cues; it is far easier to assume that neurons scattered throughout much of the hippocampus are responsive to the same cues.

This argument may also relate to an unexpected experimental result that emerged from an attempt to activate the entorhinal cortex-dentate gyrus projection using conditioned auditory cues. We were surprised to find that a very small auditory-evoked potential developed over training in virtually every location tested; by employing the technique of laminar profile analysis it was established that the responses were generated in the perforant path termination zone (Deadwyler, 1975;

Deadwyler, West, and Lynch, 1979a,b). These data strongly suggest that auditory information is distributed over a sizable portion of the dorsal hippocampus and in fact throughout the same territory containing neurons that encode spatial information. Again, this leads to the conclusion that information processing in the hippocampus does not follow anything like the topographic or segmental rules that hold for much of the nervous system.

## F    Memory Processing and the Hippocampus
To this point, we have discussed memory formation in the combinatorial network purely in terms of activity within the network. But long-term memory storage, even of the simplest representational type, appears to be peculiarly sensitive to damage in certain subcortical structures, notably the hippocampus and perhaps the dorso-medial nucleus of the thalamus (for a collection of recent reviews, see Squire and Butters, 1984). One of the reasons for selecting olfaction as a model for cortical combinatorial systems is that this modality alone has direct and well-defined connections with the dorso-medial nucleus and hippocampus; having discussed the various types of memory in combinatorial networks, it is appropriate to take up the contributions of these connections.

The effects of lesions to the hippocampal system on olfactory memory have been described (see section III.C). To reiterate, rats are able to learn to attend to smells rather than other cues, to carry out discriminations, to associate odors with reward, and to form appropriate response sequences without the entorhinal/hippocampal segments of the olfactory combinatorial chain. However, they are unable to remember specific odors for even an hour.

These results suggest that either the hippocampus itself is the site of long-term storage (with only transient memory elsewhere) or that it somehow contributes to the formation of persistent memory in other regions. This could be tested by training rats on specific and chemically similar odors *before* removing the entorhinal cortex; loss of the discrimination after the lesions would point to the conclusion that representations cannot be stored in the pyriform. If, as suggested by preliminary data (Staubli and Frasier, unpublished), rats do retain memories formed before the lesion, then the possibility that the hippocampus facilitates the encoding, storage, or usage of information in the pyriform cortex and other olfactory structures would have to be considered.

In addition to its projections into the cerebral cortex, the hippocampal formation sends axons into a variety of subcortical sites, including the septum and an area that Heimer (1978) has termed the ventral striatum. This latter region is composed of a loose collection of cell groupings that, according to Heimer, includes the nucleus accumbens septi, the olfactory tubercle, and more. Heimer argues that this zone is in actuality a ventral extension of the caudate/globus pallidus complex and is a site of reciprocal interactions between the olfactory bulb and many of its first- and second-order targets, including the pyriform/amygdala and the dorso-medial nucleus/frontal cortex, as well as the hippocampus. It is thus possible that the hippocampal representation drives cells that project back into the bulb and pyriform cortex and thereby influences the processing that occurs at those sites after the initial arrival of the odor. Smelling typically involves rapid, repetitive sampling ("sniffing"), and delayed input from the hippocampus to the ventral striatum provides a means by which the now-present odor could be coordinated with the odor experienced fractions of a second earlier (see Macrides, Eichenbaum, and Forbes, 1982, for a discussion of coordination between sniffing and hippocampal activity during olfactory learning). It is perhaps not unreasonable to suppose that these events are needed to produce a permanent record in the pyriform or bulb itself or to link a bulbar pyriform record with subcortical regions.

It is possible that the hypothesized olfactory/nonolfactory associative function of the hippocampus (see section IV.C) is linked with its role in encoding specific odor cues. In an ingenious series of experiments, Freeman (1981) and Freeman and Schneider (1982) showed that EEG activity (recorded between 64 electrodes) in the bulb changes during odor learning so that each sniff produces a reliable complex pattern of activity that is quite unlike that obtained during the first, prelearning presentation of the odor—once developed this elicited pattern is stable for at least several days. Remarkably, the learned pattern is generated even if a stimulus other than the correct one is given or if it contains no odor at all. Freeman argues that the EEG is a reflection of a "search" image sent from the brain to the bulb—that is, a neural representation of what the animal expects to smell in a particular environment. This indicates that some site in the brain has associated a representation of the odor with one for the situation and that this is relayed into the bulb. The hippocampus is an obvious candidate for this job. Using the processes described above, it provides a means by which olfactory and nonolfactory inputs could be linked and, via projections into septum, diagonal bands, and the ventral striatum, allow the nonsmell cues to trigger sniffing and at the same time project a message into the bulb. Thus, while the hippocampal associational system might not generate the recall of odors by visual and auditory stimuli (see above), it would allow such stimuli to influence smelling. Nadel, Willner, and Kurz (1985) have recently advanced a hypothesis according to which the hippocampus serves to identify the significance or context of an environment and to facilitate learning that is appropriate to it.

It would be convenient if this hippocampal influence were such as to favor high-frequency discharges by the lower levels of the olfactory projections and the production of long-term synaptic modifications. Removal of the hippocampus would then leave the animal with only short-term facilitatory processes in the pyriform, but would not necessarily impact upon previously induced synaptic changes. Presumably, however, an animal with a hippocampal lesion would not search for odors when returned to the test apparatus, and behavior would begin upon the animal's first encounter with the cue learned before the lesion.

To summarize, I am proposing that the hippocampus forms associations between olfactory and nonolfactory cues and facilitates the storage of representations of the former in extrahippocampal sites. These functions may be sequentially related; that is, development of the association allows environmental context to influence olfactory processing in a fashion appropriate for long-term memory.

## G  *The Dorso-Medial Nucleus and Memory*

While by no means compelling, there is evidence that the dorso-medial nucleus of the thalamus plays a critical role in memory formation. The afferents of the DMN are poorly understood, but, as described, one of its major subdivisions is a second-order olfactory nucleus, and lesions there certainly produce devastating impairments in smell learning. Slotnick and colleagues suggest that this is due to the loss of a capacity for forming learning sets, since lesioned rats do not improve their acquisition scores over successive problems. Eichenbaum and coworkers (Eichenbaum, Shedlack, and Eckmann, 1980; Sapolsky and Eichenbaum, 1980) argue that the problem lies in a disruption of olfactory "go/no-go" learning. These explanations are not mutually exclusive, as both imply that the rat learns something about the nature of the problem that can be used across successive discriminations (e.g., that there is a correct and an incorrect odor) and that this learning involves the DMN system. These results and interpretations point to the hypothesis that the two pathways leading out of the pyriform support or promote different kinds of memory: one involving recognition and association memory for specific odors (pyriform-hippocampal), and the other with forming response patterns and placing representations of odors within them (pyriform–dorso-medial nucleus). Without the second system the animal cannot use olfactory information in an economical fashion, and without the first it cannot build and associate representations of cues.

It is tempting to imagine that the suggested dichotomy reflects differences in anatomical organizations. The pyriform-DMN system represents a case in which an extended (cortical) combinatorial system converges upon a smaller number of cells organized as a nucleus (that is, an iterative, combinatorial system becomes a simple combinatorial system). It might be noted that recursive relationships between cortical areas and thalamic nuclei are a common feature of mammalian brains, including those of humans. The simple combinatorial step involved in cortical-thalamic connections presumably causes a considerable loss of information, since sizable percentages of neurons in the thalamus will react to more than one patterned representation. The situation is some-what different if we imagine that the thalamic nucleus provides a limited number of "states" or "commands" to its cortical targets (e.g., "go/ no-go"). These might become learned with practice with initial odor pairs so that subsequent learning would require only the matching of a given input with the appropriate "command" neurons (that is, with strengthening some synapses formed by the axons from the input array while leaving others unchanged or weakened). In the end, many representations would end on the same cells and produce the same response, something that indeed must happen somewhere in the brain with set learning. In a sense, a kind of cataloguing system would be built. Note that this would require that the DMN cells be functionally distinguished into groups by some internal (cell type) or external (different inputs) factors. Some unspecified agency would be responsible for determining which group of cells would have strengthened connections with a particular input; again, an internal signal associated with "success" (water found) or "failure" (no water) could serve this purpose. In such a system, recognition and association of signals would occur in the cortex and cortical-cortical systems, while the significance or typing of cue (in terms of responses) would reflect the operation of different subcortical nuclei.

Figure 16 summarizes the above arguments. It will be noted that the type of synaptic plasticity involved in the convergent combinatorial organization might well be different from that postulated for the iterative systems. In a nuclear organization the inputs from the representational array will not be collected into a lamina and thus will not be optimally positioned for interactions among themselves. Changes in the relative efficiency of their contacts could arise either from a widespread effect of the "typing" input or from a secondary response of the thalamic cell to that input. In either case, relatively global events in the target neuron would be triggers for plastic changes in the synapses provided by the cortical projections. This begins to resemble a "Hebbian synapse" in which modification occurs when discrete inputs are active at the same time that the recipient cell is "active."

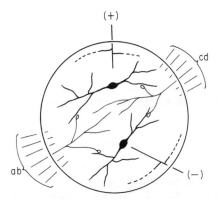

Figure 16
Hypothetical arrangements of circuitry from pyriform to dorso-medial nucleus of thalamus. Two outputs (ab and cd) from pyriform cortex enter the nucleus and each contacts the two neurons pictured. It is assumed that there is no lamination in the nucleus and the location of synapses in the dendritic trees is largely random; because of this it is further assumed that combinatorial interactions of the type postulated for cortical structures do not occur in DMN. Two subcortical projections ("+" and "−") ramify in the nucleus; these are assumed to be either quite potent and/or distributed throughout the dendrite. Changes in the strength of the pyriform connections in DMN might arise through one of two routes: (1) synchronous activity between the cortical and subcortical inputs, or (2) the cortical synapses are active when the postsynaptic cell is "active" because of prior stimulation from the subcortical projection. In this way, cortical inputs become associated with neurons defined as "+" or "−" by their subcortical afferents. The system is highly convergent in that there are many more cortical axons than target cells and therefore any DMN cell samples a large number of pyriform representations of odors. Many pyriform projections will thus activate overlapping populations of DMN cells; different odors with the same behavioral significance (+ or −) should activate the same neurons in the nucleus.

To summarize, the cortical-thalamic convergent system is argued to generate a type of memory that is quite unlike that which occurs in cortical or cortical-cortical networks. It links many cortical representations to a few, simple categories (e.g., responses) by using a type of plasticity in which near-simultaneous events in input and target alter the strength of the connections between them.

A number of cognitive psychologists have concluded that humans use two memory systems, one that stores information or data and a second that processes this according to a new set of "rules" or "procedures." The description of memory circuits provided above bears some resemblance to this dichotomization. The iterative, combinatorial arrays running through the olfactory-hippocampal network, and postulated to exist in the neocortex, were viewed as devices to store and associate representations, while the olfactory–dorso-medial nucleus convergent combinatorial system provided categorization of representations and links with specific responses. The first of these may be thought of as "data," while the second could be defined as "procedural."

## H  Circuit Patterns and Memory Types

Table II summarizes the hypothetical memory circuitries and the types of memory operations they are proposed to carry out. These involve different microanatomical arrangements and thus may employ different physiological triggers, chemical intermediates, and final forms; the pharmacological studies dissociating memory types might be pertinent to this. The list of anatomical organizations is also incomplete and, in particular, does not include subcortical to cortical nontopographic connections (the DMN to the frontal cortex, for example). These are presumably divergent though possibly still combinatorial. From the arguments posed thus far we might imagine that such arrangements are part of the "procedural" system, serving to facilitate and inhibit (select?) various cortical representations. Recursive cortical-subcortical networks of this type offer one means through which representations might be placed in sequences.

More generally, we have to assume that there are many cortical arrangements involved in memory and memory processing that do not fall into the categories described here.

Topographic memory systems are noted in the table, but lie outside the scope of this discussion. The remarkable progress being made in the extremely stereotyped nervous systems of invertebrates probably provides the best clue as to the mechanisms and operating principles used in point-to-point circuitries (for a review, see Kandel and Schwartz, 1982; Hawkins and Kandel, 1984). The work of Thompson and his collaborators (for a review, see Thompson et al., 1984) has shown that one example of conditioning involves changes in the cerebellar circuitries, and the rules so far identified might well be expected to hold true in many other topographically organized sites in the brain. How and where such sensory and motor memory systems might merge with the postulated combinatorial networks is another problem that cannot be dealt with here.

## V  Discussion

Two themes were intertwined in this review. The first took the form of an extended hypothesis about the mechanisms and circuitries used to encode memory in cortical circuitries, while the second involved a description of a system that should be useful for multidisciplinary studies of those forms of memory that predominate in the highly encephalized

Table II
Hypothetical memory circuits

| | Cortical | Cortical-Subcortical | Topographic |
|---|---|---|---|
| Circuit features | • Equal-sized input and target arrays<br>• Low level of cell-to-cell organization<br>• Laminated: different inputs collected into dendritic layers<br>• Iterative combinatorial operations with positive feedback | • Input array much larger than target array<br>• Low level of cell-to-cell organization<br>• Nuclear: inputs dispersed throughout dendrites<br>• Convergent operations | • Equal-sized input and target arrays<br>• High degree of cell-to-cell organization<br>• Nuclear: inputs spatially organized<br>• Noncombinatorial operations |
| Plasticity | • Triggered by synchronous activity in neighboring synapses<br>• Very small percentage of synapses per axon or per dendrite modified by learning episode | • Triggered by activity in disparate inputs scattered throughout dendrite—or by pre- and postsynaptic activity<br>• Significant percentage of synapses per axon in target field affected by learning episode | • Large percentage of synaptic contacts are influenced in a cell involved in a learning episode |
| Memory | • Representations of complex cues and associations are stored<br>• System has vast capacity<br>• Resembles "data" memory<br>• Involved in recognition of complex cues, association, and recall | • Simple categories of representations are constructed<br>• High capacity on input side, low capacity on output side<br>• Resembles "procedural" memory<br>• Involved in linking representations to motor acts and possibly in sequencing of representations | • Probability that a stimulus will elicit a response is changed<br>• Limited capacity<br>• Conditioning |

mammals, such as humans. A number of suggestions and predictions about memory were made during the course of the narrative, among which were the following:

- Allometric and comparative considerations suggest that combinatorial circuits are well represented throughout the cortex and hippocampus and probably other areas of the mammalian forebrain. Memory in this type of organization probably requires selective modification of synapses.
- From cellular studies of synaptic plasticity, it is known that long-lasting, selective changes in the structure, chemistry, and function of contacts are triggered by high-frequency activity occurring simultaneously or nearly simultaneously in overlapping inputs. Iterative combinatorial arrangements provide these conditions.
- Synaptic chemistries that produce essentially irreversible changes in the chemistry and perhaps the structure of synapses have been identified. Inhibitors of these processes disturb the formation of some, but not all, types of memory.
- The olfactory projections into the telencephalon provide a clear example of a series of combinatorial steps of a type that are likely to be distributed throughout the forebrain and provide a vehicle for testing the properties of such systems, particularly as they relate to memory.
- Attaching synaptic plasticity to olfactory circuitry produced several postulates about information storage in combinatorial systems. Stable representation of stimuli requires experience, and hence memory emerges as a part of perception. The experience-driven representational process allows for fragment recognition and feature detection.
- Essentially the same cellular interactions are carried out in successive combinatorial links, but their significance varies according to the position of the links in the entire chain. At lower levels they provide for representation of complex stimuli, while in later stages, where the crossing of chains can be expected, they serve to combine disparate stimuli into higher-order representations.
- The addition of feedback between higher and lower links generates recall, in which one input triggers a partial activation of the representation of a second. Similarly, connections between links in different chains provide for learned associations. These operations require circuitries that are not present in the olfactory system but are postulated to occur in the cortex.
- The hippocampus generates and stores associations between olfactory and nonolfatory stimuli; these serve to link odors to par-

ticular environmental objects and to allow environmental context to influence the processing of smells.

• The projections of the pyriform to the dorso-medial nucleus provide a convergent combinatorial system in which representations for different odors become associated with subpopulations of neurons that are "defined" by other inputs; this is postulated to provide a cataloguing system and to be responsible for something like "procedural" memory.

Though it is firmly grounded in neuroanatomy, the model remains long on speculation and short on data. It is also the case that the anatomy used in building the model was deliberately simplified, and the features ignored or minimized will eventually have to be reincorporated. Inhibition is an obvious example; it was used to regulate total activity (i.e., number of cells firing at a given time) in the combinatorial networks and for determining when and where high-frequency discharges would occur. If correct, this could still be only part of the story. The intriguing shift in the balance of extrinsic input versus associational connections noted in the pyriform through hippocampus circuitry as well as the many peculiarities associated with the dentate gyrus also deserve further investigation.

Pertinent to this, the model was presented in a purely qualitative form, which, given that many of its basic postulates are untested, seemed only sensible, but techniques are available that would provide reasonable quantitative estimates for many of the key circuit features (probability of cells interacting each other, number of contacts between an axon and a dendrite, unit EPSP, etc.). These parameters could be used to develop a more formal model and one whose behavior could be compared with various network theories of cognitive operations.

But what is most immediately needed are experimental tests of some of the more obvious predictions that emerge from the model. Here we encounter one of the great drawbacks of the olfactory system, namely, the difficulty in using odors as cues in physiological and behavioral experiments. Unlike touch, vision, and hearing, olfaction is driven by stimuli that are dispersed in time and space and do not lend themselves to categorization. These points make it very difficult to carry out physiological studies of cell firing and field potentials in behaving animals, and it is these types of data that are needed to test and extend the model. In an effort to deal with this problem, we have developed a technique in which electrodes are implanted into the olfactory bulb and electrical stimulation provides cues in a series of discriminations. The rats are first trained for several days using different pairs of odorants and then, after rapid learning of novel pairs is established, stimulation at different sites in the bulb is used for positive and negative signals. Rats did not react to single pulses delivered to the bulb, but began to sniff and in general react as though an odor was present when patterns of short high-frequency bursts were used. They learned and discriminated these simulated "odors" and remember them for very long periods (Staubli, Roman, and Lynch, 1985). This paradigm is still very much in the developmental stage, but the data collected thus far show that the technique will allow us to follow physiological events and perform tests of synaptic strength throughout the two great telencephalic pathways of the olfactory system during rapid discrimination learning and thereby test ideas about memory in cortical combinatorial systems.

It is noteworthy that patterned six/sec bursting proved to be an effective stimulus in the bulb. When we used these in the hippocampus, we found that they produced a long-term potentiation that was stable for weeks (Staubli and Lynch, unpublished). This provides evidence that at least some of the stimulation conditions used to promote LTP are psychologically meaningful. Perhaps here we begin to see a link between the requirements for synaptic change and the patterns of stimulus sampling (e.g., sniffing) used by the rat in a learning situation. Possibly the rather prosaic task of learning that stimulation of a site in the bulb leads to a reward will help us to see how synaptic biophysics and chemistry place restraints on patterns of neural activity and thus upon the design of circuitries and behavior itself. Given that a cortical system, albeit a very simple one, is being discussed here, we can imagine that answers to these questions might provide a meeting ground for the neurobiological and cognitive sciences.

*Appendix: Olfaction and Telencephalic Evolution*

The olfactory bulbs of the reptiles generate the large lateral olfactory tract that provides the dominant afferent of the anterior half of the lateral cortex; as described earlier, the lateral cortex projects densely to the remainder of the pallium and especially to the pivotal medial pallial cells. Simply on the basis of these connections we would be led to ask whether olfaction played a prominent part in the expansion of the pallium to produce the cortex, hippocampus, and related telencephalic structures. Both comparative anatomy and paleontology provide evidence in favor of this idea.

From developmental studies we know that the elaboration of sensory systems is paralleled by changes in organization of the brain, and there is good reason to suspect that the central changes are molded by the periphery. To cite but one example, mice and rats have exquisitely sensitive facial whiskers (myostacial vibrissae), for each of which is found a collection of cortical neurons arranged in an unusual barrel shape (Woolsey and van der Loos, 1970). Removal of one whisker early in postnatal life causes the dissolution of the corresponding cortical barrel; the effect of the whiskers on the cortex is mediated through a series of relay nuclei in the brain stem and thalamus (Killackey, 1980). The pervasive influence of the periphery on the brain leads inevitably to the thought that evolution of sensory systems was a major factor in determining telencephalic organization. Prominent among the differences between the earliest mammals and their Mesozoic reptilian contemporaries was the relative development of the various distance senses. Reptiles and birds have highly developed vision, but lack many of the structural specializations possessed by mammals for olfaction and hearing. Moreover, the conversion of small jawbones into middle ear bones (Hotton, 1960) as well as the appearance of bones supporting the nasal turbinates (Van Valen, 1960), specializations for hearing and smell, respectively, were found in mammallike reptiles, indicating that advances in audition and olfaction may have preceded and certainly did not follow the emergence of the mammalian telencephalon. It has been suggested that the mammals are descended from reptiles that had invaded a nocturnal niche in which odors and sounds were especially valuable signals (Jerison, 1973).[1]

It has long been thought by comparative neuroanatomists that smell played a major role in forebrain evolution simply because the primary, secondary, and many tertiary projections of the olfactory bulbs are restricted to the telencephalon. This point was illustrated in figures 8A and 8B. The lateral olfactory tract, which is composed of the axons of the mitral cells of the bulbs, forms monosynaptic connections with lateral entorhinal, pyriform, and olfactory cortices (for recent work in different species, see Haberly and Price, 1977; Skeen and Hall, 1977; Shammah-Lagnado and Nefrao, 1981); the first of these generates the massive perforant path that provides the largest afferent of the hippocampus (e.g., Hjorth-Simonsen, 1971), while the pyriform and/or olfactory cortex projects into the dorso-medial nucleus of thalamus (Price and Slotnick, 1983), the origin of the frontal cortical afferents

[1]Jerison (1973), taking note of the above points, advanced an ingenious explanation for why a greater dependence on smell and hearing would produce the increase in brain size that accompanied the emergence of the mammals. He argues that these two senses are processed in the central nervous system, with the peripheral organs serving simply as translators between physical stimulus and neuronal activity. In contrast, much visual processing is carried out in all vertebrates within the retina. While attractive, this hypothesis does not explain why different patterns of brains should appear in the birds/reptiles versus the mammals, and it does not address the differences in their allometric equations relating brain sizes to cell densities.

(Krettek and Price, 1977a, and references therein). Recent evidence indicates that these olfactory cortical regions also directly innervate frontal cortical areas (Haberly and Price, 1978a,b). Since the mitral cells are the recipients of the olfactory nerve, it follows that the frontal cortex and hippocampus are perhaps not more than 3 synapses from the odor receptors in the nasal epithelium. There is ample physiological evidence, both from electrical stimulation and behavioral studies, that supports these conclusions drawn from anatomical work (Tanabe, Iino, and Takagi, 1975; Wilson and Steward, 1978; Overmann, Woolley, and Bornschein, 1979; Habets, Lopes da Silva, and Mollevanger, 1980; Yarita et al., 1980; Macrides, Eichenbaum, and Forbes, 1982; Price and Slotnick, 1983).

The above evidence points to a large and perhaps dominant role for olfaction in telencephalic evolution, but it seems obvious that the other modalities via their thalamic projections were also involved. The cortex of even macrosmatic mammals has relatively small olfactory zones and large primary and secondary projection areas for vision, touch, and hearing. Since thalamic efferents to the pallium are present in all vertebrates, we can assume that they were present during the earliest stages of the expansion of the neocortex. Any consideration of the balance of contributions of olfactory and nonolfactory systems to cortical evolution will require considerably more comparative data, particularly on the marsupials and monotremes, than are currently in the literature. Nonetheless, some very suggestive observations have been made. The opossum has a large and well-developed dorso-medial nucleus that, in contrast to the placental mammals, is innervated across its entire extent by olfactory efferents (Benjamin et al., 1982); since the opossum is usually considered a very conservative animal, these data suggest first that the DMN was a prominent part of the early mammal thalamus, and second that it evolved as an olfactory structure. An analysis of thalamocortical connections in a monotreme (spiny anteater) produced the very intriguing results shown in figure 17 (Welker and Lende, 1980). The visual, auditory, and somatosensory areas are small and restricted to the posterior cortex, while that of the dorso-medial nucleus occupies a vast area. The anteater has very large olfactory bulbs and pyriform lobes (figure 17), so it is likely that its dorso-medial nucleus, like that of other mammals, is strongly innervated by the olfactory system. The monotremes are the most primitive of mammals, and the organization just described may hold important clues to the origins of the neocortex. Specifically, the possibility should be considered that the DMN exerted a dominant influence in the emergence of the neocortex from reptilian pallium, a scenario that would emphasize still further the role of olfaction in mammalian telencephalic evolution.

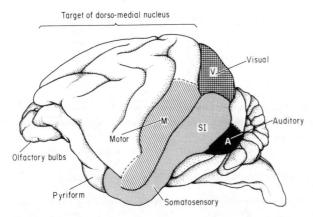

Figure 17
The brain of a monotreme (spiny anteater). The surface of the cerebral cortex and the distribution of sensory and motor regions is indicated. Note the large area innervated by the dorso-medial nucleus of the thalamus (modified from Welker and Lende, 1980).

## Acknowledgments

Michel Baudry was responsible for a great deal of the research described here and contributed significantly to the development of several of the hypotheses. Much of the biochemical and physiological work was supported by the Air Force Office of Scientific Research, while the behavioral experiments were funded by the Office of Naval Research. Preparation of this monograph would not have been possible without the patient support and encouragement of these agencies; a Research Scientist Award from the National Institutes of Health was also of great help in this regard.

## References

Aggleton, J. P., Burton, M. J., and Passingham, R. E. Cortical and subcortical afferents to the amygdala of the rhesus monkey (Macaca mulatta). *Brain Res.* 190:347–368, 1980.

Alger, B., and Nicoll, R. A. Feed forward dendritic inhibition in rat hippocampal pyramidal neurons studied *in vitro. J. Physiol.* 328:105–123, 1982.

Allen, W. F. Effect of ablating the pyriform-amygdaloid areas and hippocampi on positive and negative olfactory conditioned reflexes and on conditioned olfactory differentiation. *Amer. J. Physiol.* 132:81–91, 1941.

Andersen, P., Eccles, J. C., and Loyning, Y. Pathway of post-synaptic inhibition in hippocampus. *J. Neurophys.* 27:609–618, 1964.

Andersen, P., Sundberg, S. H., Swann J. W., and Wigstrom, H. Possible mechanisms for long-lasting potentiation of synaptic transmission in hippocampal slices from guinea pigs. *J. Physiol. Lond.* 302:463–482, 1980.

Anderson, J. R., and Bower, G. H. *Human Associative Memory*. Washington DC: V. H. Winston, 1973.

Anderson, J. A., and Hinton, G. E. Models of information processing in the brain. In G. E. Hinton and J. A. Anderson (eds.), *Parallel Models of Associative Memory*. Hillsdale, NJ: 1981, pp. 9–48.

Aoyagi, T., and Umezawa, H. Structures and activities of protease inhibitors of microbial origin. In E. Reich, E. B. Rifkin, and E. Shaw (eds.), *Proteases and Biological Control*. New York: Cold Spring Harbor, 1975, p. 429.

Barnes, C. A. Memory deficits associated with senescence; a neurophysiological and behavioral study in the rat. *J. Comp. Phys. Psychol.* 93:74–104, 1979.

Barrionuevo, G., and Brown, T. Associative long-term potentiation in hippocampal slices. *Proc. Nat. Acad. Sci. (USA)* 80:7347–7351, 1983.

Baudry, M., and Lynch, G. Regulation of glutamate receptors by cations. *Nature* 282:748–750, 1979.

Baudry, M., and Lynch, G. Regulation of hippocampal glutamate receptors: evidence for the involvement of a calcium-activated protease. *Proc. Nat. Acad. Sci.*, 77:2298–2302, 1980.

Baudry, M., and Lynch, G. Characteristics of two 3H-glutamate binding sites in rat hippocampal membranes. *J. Neurochem.* 36:811–820, 1981.

Baudry, M., Kramer, K., and Lynch, G. Irreversibility and time course of calcium stimulated 3H-glutamate binding to rat hippocampal membranes. *Brain Res.* 270:142–145, 1983.

Baudry, M., Bundman, M. C., Smith, E. K., and Lynch, G. Micromolar levels of calcium stimulates proteolytic activity and glutamate binding in rat synaptic membranes. *Science* 212:937–938, 1981.

Baudry, M., Kramer, K., Fagni, L., Recasens, M., and Lynch, G. Classification and properties of acidic amino acid receptors in hippocampus. II. Biochemical studies using a sodium efflux assay. *Molecular Pharmacology* 24:222–228, 1983.

Baudry, M., Oliver, M., Creager, R., Wierasko, A., and Lynch, G. Increase in glutamate receptors following repetitive electrical stimulation in hippocampal slices. *Life Sciences* 27:325–330, 1980.

Beckstead, R. M. Afferent connections of the entorhinal area in the rat as demonstrated by retrograde cell-labelling with horseradish peroxidase. *Brain Res.* 152:249–264, 1978.

Benjamin, R. M., Jackson, J. C., Golden, G. T., and West, C. H. K. Sources of olfactory input to opossum mediodorsal nucleus identified by horseradish peroxidase and autoradiographic methods. *J. Comp. Neurol.* 207:358–368, 1982.

Bennett, V., Davis, J., and Fowler, W. E. Brain spectrin, a membrane associated protein related in structure and function to erythrocyte spectrin. *Nature* 299:126–133, 1982.

Berger, T. W., and Thompson, R. F. Neuronal plasticity in the limbic system during classical conditioning of the rabbit nictitating membrane response. I. The hippocampus. *Brain Res.* 145:323–346, 1978.

Berger, T. W., and Thompson, R. F. Hippocampal cellular plasticity during extinction of classically conditioned nictitating membrane behavior. *Behavioral Brain Res.* 4:63–76, 1982.

Berger, T. W., Swanson, G. W., Milner, T. A., Lynch, G., and Thompson, R. F. Reciprocal anatomical connections between hippocampus and subiculum in the rabbit: evidence of subicular innervation of regio superior. *Brain Res.* 183:265–276, 1980.

Blackstad, T. W. Commissural connections of the hippocampal region in the rat with special reference to their mode of termination. *J. Comp. Neurol.* 105:417–538, 1956.

Blackstad, T. W., Brink, K., Hem, J., and Jeune, B. Distribution of hippocampal mossy fibers in the rat: an experimental study with silver impregnation methods. *J. Comp. Neurol.* 138:433–449, 1970.

Blaustein, M. P., Ratzlaff, R. W, and Schweitzer, E. S. Calcium buffering in pre-synaptic nerve terminals. II. Kinetic properties of the non-mitochondrial Ca sequestration mechanism. *J. Gen. Physiol.* 72:43–66, 1978.

Bliss, T. V. P., and Dolphin, A. C. Where is the locus of long-term potentiation? In G. Lynch, J. L. McGaugh, and N. M. Weinberger (eds.), *Neurobiology of Learning and Memory*. New York: Guilford Press, 1984, pp. 451–459.

Bliss, T. V. P., and Gardner-Medwin, A. Long-lasting potentiation of synaptic transmission in the dentate area of the unanesthetized rabbit following stimulation of the perforant path. *J. Physiol. Lond.* 232:357–374, 1973.

Bliss, T. V. P., and Lomo, T. Long-lasting potentiation of synaptic transmission in the dentate area of the anesthetized rabbit following stimulation of the perforant path. *J. Physiol. Lond.* 232:331–356, 1973.

Bok, S. T. *Histonomy of the Cerebral Cortex*. Princeton, NJ: Van Nostrand-Reinhold, 1959.

Branton, D., Cohen, C. M., and Teyler, J. Interaction of cytoskeletal proteins on human erythrocyte membrane. *Cell* 24:24–32, 1981.

Broadwell, R. D. Olfactory relationships of the telencephalon and diencephalon in the rabbit. I. An autoradiographic study of the efferent connections of the main and accessory olfactory bulbs. *J. Comp. Neurol.* 163:329–346, 1975.

Brown, T. H., and McAfee, D. A. Long-term synaptic potentiation in the superior cervical ganglion. *Science* 215:1411–1413, 1982.

Burridge, K., Kelly, T., and Mangeat, M. Nonerythrocyte spectrins: actin-membrane attachment proteins occurring in many cell types. *J. Cell Biol.* 95:478, 1982.

Cajal, S. R. *Histologie du Systeme Nerveux de l'Homme et des Vertebres*, Vol. II. Paris: Maluine, 1911.

Carlin, R. K., Bartelt, D. C., and Siekevitz, P. Identification of fodrin as a major calmodulin-binding protein in postsynaptic density preparations. *J. Cell Biol.* 96:443–448, 1983.

Carlsen, J., De Olmos, J., and Heimer, L. Tracing of two-neuron pathways in the olfactory system by the aid of transneuronal degeneration: projections to the amygdaloid body and hippocampal formation. *J. Comp. Neur.* 208:196–208, 1982.

Chang, F.-L. F., and Greenough, W. T. Transient and enduring morphological correlates of synaptic activity and efficacy change in the rat hippocampal slice. *Brain Res.* 309:35–46, 1984.

Cohen, N., and Squire, L. R. Perserved learning and retention of pattern analyzing skill in amnesia: dissociation of knowing how and knowing that. *Science* 210:207–209, 1980.

Cooper, L. N., Lieberman, F., and Oja, E. A theory for the acquisition and loss of neuron specificity in visual cortex. *Biol. Cybernetics* 33:9–28, 1979.

Crain, B., Cotman, C., Taylor, D., and Lynch, G. A quantitative electron microscopic study of synaptogenesis in the dentate gyrus of the rat. *Brain Res.* 63:195–204, 1973.

Dayton, W. R., Schollmeyer, J. V., Lepley, R. A., and Cortex, L. R. A calcium-activated protease possibly involved in myofibrillar protein turnover: isolation of a low-calcium-requiring form of the protease. *Biochim. Biophys. Acta* 659:48–61, 1981.

Deadwyler, S. A., West, M., and Lynch, G. Activity of dentate granule cells during learning: differentiation of perforant path input. *Brain Res.* 169:29–43, 1979a.

Deadwyler, S. A., West, M., and Lynch, G. Synaptically identified hippocampal slow potentials during behavior. *Brain Res.* 161:211–225, 1979b.

Deadwyler, S. A., West, J., Cotman, C. W., and Lynch, G. Physiological studies of the reciprocal connection between hippocampus and entorhinal cortex. *Exp. Neur.* 49:35, 1975.

de la Baume, S., Yi, C. C., Schwartz, J. C., Marcaise-Collado, H., and Constentin, J. Participation of both 'enkephalinase' and aminopeptidase activities in the metabolism of endogenous enkephalins. *Neuroscience* 8:143–153, 1983.

De Martino, G. N. Calcium dependent proteolytic activity in rat liver: identification of two proteases with different calcium requirements. *Arch. Biochem. Biophys.* 253–257, 1981.

DiChiara, G., and Gessa, G. L. *Glutamate as a Neurotransmitter.* New York: Raven Press, 1980.

Douglas, R. M. Long lasting synaptic potentiation in the rat dentate gyrus following brief high frequency stimulation. *Brain Res.* 361–365, 1977.

Douglas, R. M., and Goddard, G. Long-term potentiation of the perforant path-granule cell synapses in the rat hippocampus. *Brain Res.* 86:205–215, 1975.

Douglas, R. M., Goddard, G. V., and Riives, M. Inhibitory modulation of long-term potentiation: evidence for a postsynaptic locus of control. *Brain Res.* 240:259–272, 1982.

Dunlop, D. S., Van Elden, W., and Lajtha, A. Protein degradation rates in regions of the central nervous system *in vivo* during development. *Biochem. J.* 170:637–642, 1978.

Dunwiddie, T., and Lynch, G. Long-term potentiation and depression of synaptic responses in the rat hippocampus: Localization and frequency dependency. *J. Physiol. Lond.* 276:353–367, 1978.

Dunwiddie, T. V., and Lynch, G. The relationship between extracellular calcium concentrations and the induction of hippocampal long-term potentiation. *Brain Res.* 169:103–110, 1979.

Dunwiddie, T., Madison, D. V., and Lynch, G. Synaptic transmission is required for the initiation of long-term potentiation. *Brain Res.* 150:413–417, 1978.

Eccles, J. C. Calcium in long-term potentiation as a model for memory. *Neuroscience* 10:1071–1081, 1983.

Eichenbaum, H., Clegg, R. A., and Feeley, A. Reexamination of functional subdivisions of the rodent prefrontal cortex. *Exp. Neurol.* 79:434–451, 1983.

Eichenbaum, H., Shedlack, K. J., and Eckmann, K. W. Thalmocortical mechanisms in odor-guided behavior. I. Effects of lesions of the mediodorsal thalamic nucleus and frontal cortex on olfactory discrimination in the rat. *Brain Behav. Evol.* 17:255–275, 1980.

Eichenbaum, H., Morton, T. H., Potter, H., and Corkin, S. Selective olfactory deficits in case H.M. *Brain* 106:459–472, 1983.

Fagg, G. E., and Matus, A. Selective association of N-methyl-aspartate and quisqualate types of L-glutamate receptors with brain postsynaptic densities. *Proc. Nat. Acad. Sci. (USA)* 81:6876–6880, 1984.

Feldman, J. A. A connectionist model of visual memory. In G. E. Hinton and J. A. Anderson (eds.), *Parallel Models of Associative Memory.* Hillsdale, NJ: Lawrence Erlbaum, 1981, pp. 49–82.

Fifková, E., and Delay, R. Cytoplasmic actin in neuronal processes as a possible mediator of synaptic plasticity. *J. Cell Biol.* 95:345–350, 1982.

Fifková, E., Markham, J. A., and Delay, R. J. Calcium in the spine aparatus of dendritic spines in the dentate molecular layer. *Brain Res.* 266:163–168, 1983.

Flood, J. F., Bennett, E. L., Orme, A. E., and Rosenzweig, M. R. Memory: modification of anisomyocin induced amnesia by stimulants and depressants. *Science* 199:324–326, 1978.

Flood, J. F., Jarvik, M. E., Bennett, E. L., Orme, A. E., and Rosenzweig, M. R. The effect of stimulants, depressants, and protein synthesis inhibition on retention. *Behav. Biol.* 20:168–183, 1977.

Freedman, J., and Haber, R. N. One reason why we rarely forget a face. *Bull. Psychonomic Society* 3:2, 1974.

Freeman, W. J. A physiological hypothesis of perception. *Perspectives in Biology and Medicine* 561–592, 1981.

Freeman, W. J., and Schneider, W. Changes in spatial patterns of rabbit olfactory EEG with conditioning to odors. *Psychophysiology* 19:44–56, 1982.

Gall, C., and Lynch, G. The regulation of fiber growth and synaptogenesis in the developing hippocampus. In R. K. Hunt (ed.), *Current Topics in Developmental Biology*, Vol. 15. New York: Academic Press, 1980, pp. 159–180.

Gazzaniga, M. Cognitive neuroscience: more plain talk. In Fritz Machlup and Una Mansfield (eds.), *The Study of Information*. New York: John Wiley, 1983.

Glenney, J. R., and Glenney, P. Fodrin is the general spectrin-like protein found in most cells whereas spectrin and the TW protein have a restricted distribution. *Cell* 34:503–512, 1983.

Glenney, J. R., Glenney, P., and Weber, K. Erythroid spectrin, brain fodrin, and intestinal brush border proteins (TW-260/240) are related molecules containing a common calmodulin-binding subunit bound to a variant cell type-specific subunit. *Proc. Nat. Acad. Sci. (USA)* 79:4002–4005, 1982a.

Glenney, J. R., Glenney, P., and Weber, K. F-actin-binding and cross-linking properties of porcine brain fodrin, a spectrin-related molecule. *J. Biol. Chem.* 257:9781–9787, 1982b.

Gold, P. E., and Sternberg, D. B. Retrograde amnesia produced by several treatments: evidence for a common biological mechanism. *Science* 201:367–369, 1978.

Goodman, S. R., and Shiffer, K. The spectrin membrane skeleton of normal and abnormal human erythrocytes: a review. *Am. J. Physiol.* 244:c121–c124, 1983.

Graziadei, P. P. C., and Monti-Graziadei, G. Continuous nerve cell renewal in the olfactory system. In *Handbook of Sensory Physiology IX*. New York: Springer-Verlag, 1978, pp. 55–83.

Greenough, W. Structural correlates of information storage in mammalian brain: a review and hypothesis. *Trends in Neurosci.* 7:229–233, 1984.

Guroff, G. A neutral, calcium-activated proteinase from the soluble fraction of rat brain. *J. Biol. Chem.* 239:149–155, 1964.

Habeles, M. *Local Cortical Networks*. New York: Springer, 1982.

Haberly, L. B., and Price, J. L. The axonal projection patterns of the mitral and tufted cells of the olfactory bulb in the rat. *Brain Res.* 129:152–157, 1977.

Haberly, L. B., and Price, J. L. Association and commissural fiber systems of the olfactory cortex of the rat. I. Systems originating in the piriform cortex and adjacent areas. *J. Comp. Neurol.* 178:711–740, 1978a.

Haberly, L. B., and Price, J. L. Association and commissural fiber systems of the olfactory cortex of the rat. II. Systems originating in the olfactory peduncle. *J. Comp. Neurol.* 181:781–808, 1978b.

Haberly, L. B., and Shepherd, G. M. Current-density analysis of summed evoked potentials in the opossum prepyriform cortex. *J. Neurophysiol.* 36:789–802, 1973.

Habets, A. M. M. C., Lopes da Silva, F. H., and Mollevanger, W. J. An olfactory input to the hippocampus of the cat: field potential analysis. *Brain Res.* 182:47–64, 1980.

Hatanaka, M., Yoshimura, N., Murakami, T., Kannagi, R., and Murachi, T. Evidence for membrane-associated calpain I in human erythrocytes: detection by an immuno-electrophoretic blotting method using monospecific antibody. *Biochem.* 23:3272–3278, 1984.

Hawkins, R. D., and Kandel, E. R. Steps toward a cell-biological alphabet for elementary forms of learning. In G. Lynch, N. Weinberger, and J. McGaugh (eds.), *Neurobiology of Learning and Memory*. New York: Guilford Press, 1984, pp. 385–404.

Hebb, D. O. *The Organization of Behavior*. New York: Wiley, 1949.

Heimer, L. The olfactory cortex and the ventral striatum. In M. Livingston and H. Hor-nykiewicz (eds.), *Limbic Mechanisms*. New York: Plenum, 1978, pp. 95–187.

Hinton, G. E., and Anderson, J. A. *Parallel Models of Associative Conditioning*. Hillsdale, NJ: Lawrence Erlbaum, 1981.

Hirokawa, N., Cheney, R. E., and Willard, M. Location of a protein of the fodrin-spectrin-TW 260/240 family in the mouse intestinal brush border. *Cell* 32:953–965, 1983.

Hjorth-Simonsen, A. Hippocampal efferents to the ipsilateral entorhinal area: an experimental study in the rat. *J. Comp. Neurol.* 142:417–438, 1971.

Hjorth-Simonsen, A. Projections of the lateral part of the hippocampus and fascia dentata. *J. Comp. Neurol.* 146:219–232, 1972.

Hjorth-Simonsen, A., and Jeune, B. Origin and termination of the hippocampal perforant path in the rat studied by silver impregnation. *J. Comp. Neurol.* 144:215–232, 1972.

Hopson, J. A. Paleoneurology. In C. C. Gans, R. G. Northcutt, and P. S. Ulinsky, (eds.), *Biology of the Reptilia*, Vol. 9. London: Academic Press, 1979, pp. 39–146.

Hotton, N., III. The chorda tympani and middle ear as guides to origin and divergence of reptiles. *Evolution* 14:194–211, 1960.

Jerison, H. J. *Evolution of the Brain and Intelligence*. New York: Academic Press, 1973.

Jinbu, Y., Sato, S., Nakao, M., Tsukita, S., Tsukita, S., and Ishikawa, H. The role of ankyrin in shape and deformability change of human erythrocyte ghosts. *Biochim. Biophys. Acta* 773:237–245, 1984.

Jones, B. P., Moskowitz, H. R., and Butters, N. Olfactory discrimination in alcoholic Korsakoff patients. *Neuropsychologia* 13:173–179, 1975.

Jourdan, F. Spatial dimension in olfactory coding: a representation of the 2-deoxyglucose patterns of glomerular labeling in the olfactory bulb. *Brain Res.* 240:341–344, 1982.

Jourdan, F., Dubeau, A., Astic, L., and Holley, A. Spatial distribution of [14C]2-deoxyglucose uptake in the olfactory bulbs of rats stimulated with two different odours. *Brain Res.* 188:139–154, 1980.

Kandel, E. R., and Schwartz, J. H. Molecular biology of learning: modulation of transmitter release. *Science* 218:433–443, 1982.

Kandel, E. R., Spencer, W. A., and Brinley, F. J. Electrophysiology of hippocampal neurons. I. Sequential invasion and synaptic organization. *J. Neurophys.* 24:225–242, 1961.

Kay, M. M. B., Tracey, C. M., Goodman, J. R., Cone, J. C., and Bassel, P. S. Polypeptides immunologically related to band 3 are present in nucleated somatic cells. *Proc. Nat. Acad. Sci.* 80:6882–6886, 1983.

Kelso, S. R., and Brown, T. H. Differential induction of associative LTP. *Soc. Neurosci. Abstr.* 11:780, 1985.

Killackey, H. P. Pattern formation in the trigeminal system of the rat. *Trends Neuroscience* 3:303–306, 1980.

Kishimoto, A., Kajikawa, N., Tabuchi, H., Shiota, M., and Nishizuka, Y. Calcium-dependent neutral protease: widespread occurrence of a species of protease active at lower concentrations of calcium. *J. Biochem.* 90:892–899, 1981.

Klein, I., Lehotay, D., and Godek, M. Characterization of a calcium-activated proteinase that hydrolyzes a microtubule-associated protein. *Archives. Biochem. Biophys.* 208:520–527, 1981.

Kohonen, T., Oja, E., and Lehtiö, P. Storage and processing of information in distributed associative memory systems. In G. E. Hinton and J. A. Anderson (eds.), *Parallel Models of Associative Memory*. Hillsdale, NJ: Lawrence Erlbaum, 1981, pp. 105–143.

Kosel, K. C., Van Hoesen, G. W., and Rosene, D. L. Non-hippocampal cortical projections from the entorhinal cortex in the rat and rhesus monkey. *Brain Res.* 244:201–213, 1982.

Kosel, K. C., Van Hoesen, G. W., and West, J. R. Olfactory bulb projections to the parahippocampal area of the rat. *J. Comp. Neur.* 198:467–482, 1981.

Krettek, J. E., and Price, J. L. The cortical projections of the mediodorsal nucleus and adjacent thalamic nuclei in the rat. *J. Comp. Neurol.* 171:157–192, 1977a.

Krettek, J. E., and Price, J. L. Projections from the amygdaloid complex and adjacent olfactory structures to the entorhinal cortex and the subiculum in the rat and cat. *J. Comp. Neurol.* 172:723–752, 1977b.

Lancet, D., Greer, C. A., Kauer, J. S., and Shepherd, G. M. Mapping of odor-related neuronal activity in the olfactory bulb by high-resolution 2-deoxyglucose autoradiography. *Proc. Nat. Acad. Sci.* 79:670–674, 1982.

Landis, D. M. D., and Reese, T. S. Cytoplasmic organization in cerebellar dendritic spines. *J. Cell Biol.* 97:1169–1178, 1983.

Larson, J., Wong, D., and Lynch, G. Patterned stimulation at the theta frequency is optimal for the induction of hippocampal long-term potentiation. *Brain Res.* (in press).

Laurberg, S., and Sorensen, K. E. Associational and commissural collaterals of neurons in the hippocampal formation (Hilus fasciae dentatae and subfield CA3). *Brain Res.* 212:287–300, 1981.

Lazarides, E., and Nelson, W. J. Expression of spectrin in nonerythroid cells. *Cell* 31:505–508, 1982.

Lazarides, E., and Nelson, W. J. Erythrocyte form of spectrin in cerebellum: appearance at a specific stage in the terminal differentiation of neurons. *Science* 222:931–933, 1983.

Lee, K. S. Sustained enhancement of evoked potentials following brief, high-frequency stimulation of the cerebral cortex in vitro. *Brain Res.* 239:617–623, 1982.

Lee, K. S. Cooperativity among afferents for the induction of long-term potentiation in the CA1 region of the hippocampus. *J. Neuroscience* 3:1369–1372, 1983.

Lee, K., Oliver, M., Schottler, F., and Lynch, G. Electron microscopic studies of brain slices: the effects of high frequency stimulation on dendritic ultrastructure. In G. Kerkut and H. V. Wheal (eds.), *Electrical Activity in Isolated Mammalian C.N.S. Preparations.* New York: Academic Press, 1981, pp. 189–212.

Lee, K., Schottler, F., Oliver, M., and Lynch, G. Brief bursts of high frequency stimulation produce two types of structural changes in rat hippocampus. *J. Neurophysiol.* 44:247–258, 1980.

Lende, R. A. Representation in the cerebral cortex of a primitive mammal: sensorimotor, visual, and auditory fields in the echidna (Tachyglossus aculeatus). *J. Neurophys.* 27:37, 1964.

Levine, J., and Willard, M. Fodrin: axonally transported polypeptide associated with the internal periphery of many cells. *J. Cell Biol.* 90:631–643, 1981.

Levine, J., and Willard, M. Redistribution of fodrin (a component of the cortical cytoplasm) accompanying capping of cell surface molecules. *Proc. Nat. Acad. Sci. (USA)* 80:191–195, 1983.

Levy, W. B., and Steward, O. Synapses as associative memory elements in the hippocampal formation. *Brain Res.* 175:233–245, 1979.

Libby, P., and Goldberg, A. L. Leupeptin, a protease inhibitor, decreases protein degradation in normal and diseased muscle. *Science* 199:534, 1978.

Lohman, A. H. M., and Mentink, G. M. Some cortical connections of the tegu lizard (Tupinambis tequixin). *Brain Res.* 45:325–344, 1972.

Lohman, A. H. M., and Van Woerden-Verkley, I. Further studies on the cortical connections of the tegu lizard. *Brain Res.* 103:9–23, 1976.

Lorente de Nó, R. Studies on the structure of the cerebral cortex. II. Continuation of the study of the ammonic system. *J. Psycholigie and Neurologie* 19:113–177, 1934.

Luskin, M. B., and Price, J. L. The distribution of axon collaterals from the olfactory bulb and the nucleus of the horizontal limb of the diagonal band to the olfactory cortex, demonstrated by double retrograde labelling techniques. *J. Comp. Neurol.* 209:249–263, 1983a.

Luskin, M. B., and Price, J. L. The laminar distribution of intracortical fibers originating in the olfactory cortex of the rat. *J. Comp. Neurol.* 216:292–302, 1983b.

Lynch, G., and Baudry, M. The biochemistry of memory: a new and specific hypothesis. *Science* 224:1057–1063, 1984.

Lynch, G. S., Dunwiddie, T., and Gribkoff, V. Heterosynaptic depression: a correlate of long term potentiation. *Nature* 266:737–739, 1977.

Lynch, G., Halpain, S., and Baudry, M. Effects of high-frequency stimulation on glutamate receptor binding studied with a modified in vitro hippocampal slice preparation. *Brain Res.* 244:101–111, 1982.

Lynch, G, Larson, J., and Baudry, M. Proteases, neuronal stability, and brain aging: an hypothesis. In R. Barkus and T. Crooke (eds.), *Treatment Development Strategies for Alzheimer's Disease* (in press).

Lynch, G., Rose, G., and Gall, C. Anatomical and functional aspects of the septo-hippocampal system. In L. Weiskrantz and J. Gray (eds.), *The Septo-Hippocampal System*. London: CIBA, 1978, pp. 5–24.

Lynch, G., Smith, R. L., Mensah, P., and Cotman, C. Tracing the dentate gyrus mossy fiber system with horseradish peroxidase histochemistry. *Exp. Neurol.* 40:516–524, 1973.

Lynch, G., Jensen, R. A., McGaugh, J. L., Davila, K., and Oliver, M. Effects of enkephalin, morphine, and naloxone on the electrical activity of the hippocampal slice preparation. *Exp. Neurol.* 71:527–540, 1981.

Lynch, G., Larson, J., Kelso, S., Barrionuevo, G., and Schottler, F. Intracellular injections of EGTA block the induction of hippocampal long-term potentiation. *Nature* 305:719–721, 1983.

McCormick, D. A., Clark, G. A., Lavond, D. G., and Thompson, R. F. Initial localization of the memory trace for a basic form of learning. *Proc. Nat. Acad. Sci. (USA)* 79:2737, 1982.

McNaughton, B. L., Douglas, R. M., and Goddard, G. V. Synaptic enhancement in fascia dentata: cooperativity among coactive afferents. *Brain Res.* 157:277–293, 1978.

Macrides, F., Eichenbaum, H. B., and Forbes, W. B. Temporal relationship between sniffing and the limbic (theta) rhythm during odor discrimination reversal learning. *J. Neuroscience* 2:1705–1717, 1982.

McWilliams, J. R., and Lynch, G. Terminal proliferation and synaptogenesis following partial deafferentation: the reinnervation of the inner molecular layer of the dentate gyrus following removal of its commissural afferents. *J. Comp. Neurol.* 180:581–615, 1978.

McWilliams, J. R., and Lynch, G. Terminal proliferation in the partially deafferented dentate gyrus: time course for the appearance and removal of degeneration and the replacement of lost terminals. *J. Comp. Neurol.* 187:191–198, 1979.

Mamounas, L., Thompson, R. F., Lynch, G., and Baudry, M. Classical conditioning of rabbit eyelid responses increases glutamate receptor binding in hippocampal synaptic membranes. *Proc. Nat. Acad. Sci. (USA)* 81:2478–2482, 1984.

Marchesi, V. T. Spectrin: present status of a putative cyto-skeletal protein of the red cell membrane. *J. Membrane Biol.* 51:101–131, 1979.

Matthews, D. A., Cotman, C. W., and Lynch, G. An electron microscopic study of lesion-induced synaptogenesis in the dentate gyrus of the adult rat. I. Magnitude and time course of degeneration. *Brain Res.* 115:1–22, 1976a.

Matthews, D. A., Cotman, C. W., and Lynch, G. An electron microscopic study of lesion-induced synaptogenesis in the dentate gyrus of the adult rat. II. Reappearance of morphologically normal synaptic contacts. *Brain Res.* 115:23–41, 1976b.

Mellegren, R. L. Canine cardiac calcium-dependent proteases: resolution of two forms with different requirements for calcium. *FEBS Lett.* 109:129–133, 1980.

Melloni, E., Sparatore, B., Salamino, F., Michetti, M., and Pontremoli, S. Cytosolic calcium dependent proteinase of human erythrocytes: formation of an enzyme-natural inhibitor complex induced by Ca2+ ions. *Biochem. Biophys. Res. Commun.* 106:731–740, 1982.

Mishkin, M., Malamut, B., and Bachevalier, J. Memories and habits: two neural systems. In G. Lynch, J. L. McGaugh, and N. M. Weinberger (eds.), *Neurobiology of Learning and Memory*. New York: Guilford Press, 1984, pp. 65–78.

Morris, M. E., Krnjevic, K., and Ropert, N. Changes in free Ca2+ recorded inside hippocampal pyramidal neurons in response to fimbrial stimulation. *Society for Neuroscience* (Abstract) 9:395, 1983.

Mosko, S., Lynch, G., and Cotman, C. The distribution of the septal projections to the hippocampus of the rat. *J. Comp. Neur.* 152:163–174, 1973.

Murachi, T., Tanaka, K., Hatanaka, M., and Murakami, T. Intracellular Ca$^{++}$-dependent protease (calpain) and its high molecular weight endogenous inhibitor (calpastatin). *Advances in Enzyme Regulation* 19:407–419, 1981a.

Murachi, T., Hatanaka, M., Yasumoto, Y., Nakayama, N., and Tanaka, T. Quantitative distribution study on calpain and calpastatin in rat tissues and cells. *Biochem. Inter.* 2:651–656, 1981b.

Nadel, L., Willner, J., and Kurz, E. M. Cognitive maps and environmental context. In P. D. Balsam and A. Tomic (eds.), *Context and Learning.* Hillsdale, NJ: Lawrence Erlbaum 1985, pp. 385–406.

Nelson, W. J., Colaco, C. A. L. S., and Lazarides, E. Involvement of spectrin in cell-surface receptor capping in lymphocytes. *Proc. Natl. Acad. Sci. (USA)* 80:1626–1630, 1983.

Nigrosh, B. J., Slotnick, B. M., and Nevin, J. A. Olfactory discrimination, reversal learning, and stimulus control in rats. *J. Comp. Physiol. Psych.* 89:285–294, 1975.

Northcutt, R. G. Evolution of telencephalon in non-mammalian vertebrates. *Ann. Rev. Neurosci.* 4:301–350, 1981.

O'Keefe, J. Place units in the hippocampus of the freely moving rat. *Exp. Neurol.* 51:78–109, 1976.

O'Keefe, J., and Nadel, L. *The Hippocampus as a Cognitive Map.* London: Oxford University Press, 1978.

Overmann, S. R., Woolley, D. E., and Bornschein, R. L. Hippocampus potentials evoked by stimulation of olfactory basal forebrain and lateral septum in the rat. *Brain Res. Bull.* 5:437–449, 1979.

Palek, J., Stewart, G., and Lionetti, F. J. The dependence of shape of erythrocyte ghosts on calcium, magnesium, and adenosine triphosphate. *Blood* 44:583–597, 1974.

Palm, G. Rules for synaptic changes and their relevance for the storage of information in the brain. In R. Trappel (ed.), *Cybernetics and Systems Research.* North Holland: Elsevier, 1982, pp. 277–280.

Perkel, D. H., and Perkel, D. J. Dendritic spines: role of active membrane in modulating synaptic efficacy. *Brain Res.* 325:331–335, 1985.

Pinching, A. J., and Doving, K. B. Selective degeneration in the rat olfactory bulb following exposure to different odours. *Brain Res.* 82:195–204, 1974.

Potter, H., and Butters, N. An assessment of olfactory deficits in patients with damage to prefrontal cortex. *Neuropsychologia* 18:621–628, 1980.

Price, J. L. An autoradiographic study of complementary laminar patterns of termination of afferent fibers to the olfactory cortex. *J. Comp. Neur.* 150:87–108, 1973.

Price, J. L., and Slotnick, B. M. Dual olfactory representation in the rat thalamus: an anatomical and electrophysiological study. *J. Comp. Neurol.* 215:63–77, 1983.

Quiroga, J. C. The brain of two mammal-like reptiles (Cynodontia-Therapsida). *J. Hirnforsch.* 20:341–350, 1979.

Racine, R. J., and Milgram, N. W. Short-term potentiation phenomena in the rat limbic forebrain. *Brain Res.* 260:201–216, 1983.

Racine, R. J., Milgram, N. W., and Hafner, S. Long-term potentiation phenomena in the rat limbic forebrain. *Brain Res.* 260:217–231, 1983.

Raisman, G., Cowan, W. M., and Powell, T. P. S. The extrinsic afferent, commissural, and association fibers of the hippocampus. *Brain Res.* 88:963–996, 1965.

Ralston, G. B. The structure of spectrin and the shape of the red blood cell. *Trends Biochem. Sci.* 3:195–198, 1978.

Robinson, H., and Koch, C. An information storage mechanism: calcium and spines. A. I. Memo 779 (MIT), 1984, pp. 1–13.

Rose, G., and Schubert, P. Release and transfer of [3H] adenosine derivatives in the cholinergic septal system. *Brain Res.* 121:353–357, 1977.

Rosene, D. L., and Van Hoesen, G. W. Hippocampal afferents reach widespread areas of cerebral cortex and amygdala in the rhesus monkey. *Science* 198:315–317, 1977.

Salpeter, M., Leonard, J. P., and Kasprzak, M. Agonist-induced postsynaptic myopathy. *Neuroscience Commentaries* 1:73–83, 1982.

Sandoval, I. V., and Weber, K. Calcium-induced inactivation of microtubule formation in brain extracts. *Eur. J. Biochem.* 92:463, 1978.

Sapolsky, R. M., and Eichenbaum, H. Thalmocortical mechanisms in odor-guided behavior. II. Effects of lesions of the mediodorsal thalamic nucleus and frontal cortex on odor preferences and sexual behavior in the hamster. *Brain Behav. Evol.* 17:276–290, 1980.

Sasaki, T., Yoshimura, N., Kikuchi, T., Hananaka, M., Kitahara, A., Sakibama, T., and Murachi, T. Similarity and dissimilarity in subunit structures of calpains I and II from various sources as demonstrated by immunological cross-reactivity. *J. Biochem.* 94:2055–2061, 1983.

Savage, D. D., Werling, L. L., Nadler, J. V., and McNamara, J. O. Selective increase in L-[3H]glutamate binding to a quisqualate-sensitive site on hippocampal synaptic membranes after angular bundle kindling. *Europ. J. Pharmacol.* 85:255–256, 1982.

Schlaepfer, W. W., and Hasler, M. B. Characterization of the calcium-induced disruption of neurofilaments in rat peripheral nerve. *Brain Res.* 168:299–309, 1979.

Schlaepfer, W. W., and Micko, S. Chemical and structural changes of neurofilaments in rat sciatic nerve. *J. Cell Biol.* 78:369–378, 1978.

Schwartz, S. P., and Coleman, P. D. Neurons of origin of the perforant path. *Exp. Neurol.* 74:305–312, 1981.

Schwob, J. E., and Price, J. L. The cortical projection of the olfactory bulb: development in fetal and neonatal rats correlated with quantitative variations in adult rats. *Brain Res.* 151:369–374, 1978.

Scott, J. W., McBridge, R. L., and Schneider, S. P. The organization of projections from the olfactory bulb to piriform cortex and olfactory tubercle in the rat. *J. Comp. Neurol.* 194:519–534, 1980.

Seifert, W. (ed.). *Neurobiology of the Hippocampus.* New York: Academic Press, 1983.

Shammah-Lagnado, S. J., and Nefrao, N. Efferent connections of the olfactory bulb in the oppossum (Didelphis marsupialis aurita): a Fink-Heimer study. *J. Comp. Neurol.* 201:51–63, 1981.

Sharif, G. A. Cell counts in primate cerebral cortex. *J. Comp. Neurol.* 98:381–400, 1953.

Siekevitz, P. The postsynaptic density: a possible role in long lasting effects in the central nervous system. *Proc. Nat. Acad. Sci. (USA)* 82:2494–3498, 1985.

Siman, R., Baudry, M., and Lynch, G. Purification from synaptosomal plasma membranes of calpain I, a thiol- protease activated by micromolar calcium concentrations. *J. Neurochem.* 41:950–956, 1983.

Siman, R., Baudry, M., and Lynch, G. Brain fodrin: substrate for calpain I, an endogenous calcium-activated protease. *Proc. Nat. Acad. Sci. (USA)* 81:3276–3280, 1984.

Siman, R., Baudry, M., and Lynch, G. Calcium-activated proteases as possible mediators of synaptic plasticity. In: G. Edelman, W. M. Cowan, and W. E. Gall (eds.), *Dynamic Aspects of Neocortical Function.* New York: Wiley, 1985a (in press).

Siman, R., Baudry, M., and Lynch, G. Glutamate receptor regulation by proteolysis of the cytoskeletal protein fodrin. *Nature* 315:225–227, 1985b.

Simonson, L., Baudry, M., Siman, R., and Lynch, G. Regional distribution of soluble calcium activated proteolytic activity in neonatal and adult rat brain. *Brain Res.* 327:153–159, 1985.

Skeen, L. C., and Hall, W. C. Efferent projections of the main and accessory olfactory bulb in the tree shrew (Tupaia glis). *J. Comp. Neurol.* 172:1–36, 1977.

Slotnick, B. M., and Kaneko, N. Role of mediodorsal thalamic nucleus in olfactory discrimination learning in rats. *Science* 214:91–92, 1981.

Slotnick, B. M., and Katz, H. M. Olfactory learning-set formation in rats. *Science* 185:796–798, 1974.

Smith, D. O., and Westheimer, J. L. Decreased sprouting and degeneration of nerve terminals of active muscles in aged rats. *J. Neurophys.* 48:101–109, 1982.

Sorensen, K. E., and Shipley, K. T. Projections from the subiculum to the deep layers of the ipsilateral presubicular and entorhinal cortices in the guinea pig. *J. Comp. Neurol.* 188:313–334, 1979.

Squire, L. R. The neuropsychology of human memory. *Ann. Rev. Neuroscience* 5:241–273, 1982.

Squire, L. R., and Barondes, S. H. Anisomycin, like other inhibitors of cerebral protein synthesis, impairs long-term memory of a discrimination task. *Brain Res.* 66:301–308, 1974.

Squire, L. R., and Butters, N. (eds.). *Neuropsychology of Memory.* New York: Guilford Press, 1984.

Squire, L. R., Cohen, N. J., and Nadel, L. The medial temporal region and memory consolidation: a new hypothesis. In H. Weingartner and E. Parder (eds.), *Memory Consolidation.* Hillsdale, NJ: Erlbaum, 1985, pp. 185–209.

Standing, L. Learning 10,000 pictures. *Quart. J. Exp. Psych.* 25:207–222, 1973.

Staubli, U., Baudry, M., and Lynch, G. Leupeptin, a thiol proteinase inhibitor, causes a selective impairment of maze performance in rats. *Behavioral and Neural Biology* 40:48–69, 1984.

Staubli, U., Baudry, M., and Lynch, G. Olfactory discrimination learning is blocked by leupeptin, a thiol-proteinase inhibitor. *Brain Res.* 337:333–336, 1985.

Staubli, U., Faraday, R., and Lynch, G. Pharmacological dissociation of memory: anisomycin, and leupeptin selectively disrupt different memory tasks. *Behav. and Neural Biology* 43:287–297, 1985.

Staubli, U., Ivy, G., and Lynch, G. Denervation of hippocampus causes rapid forgetting of olfactory memory in rats. *Proc. Nat. Acad. Sci. (USA)* 81:5885–5887, 1985.

Staubli, U., Roman, F., and Lynch, G. Selective changes in synaptic responses elicited in a cortical network by behaviorally relevant electrical stimulation. *Soc. Neurosci. Abstr.* 11:837, 1985.

Steck, T. L. The organization of proteins in the human red blood cell membrane. *J. Cell Biol.* 62:1–19, 1974.

Steward, O. Topographic organization of the projections from the entorhinal area to the hippocampal formation of the rat. *J. Comp. Neurol.* 167:285–314, 1976.

Steward, O., and Scoville, S. A. Cells of origin of entorhinal cortical afferents to the hippocampus and fascia dentata of the rat. *J. Comp. Neurol.* 169:347–370, 1976.

Stewart, W. B., Kauer, J. S., and Shepherd, G. M. Functional organization of rat olfactory bulb analysed by the 2-deoxyglucose method. *J. Comp. Neurol.* 185:715–734, 1979.

Swanson, L. W. A direct projection from Ammon's horn to prefrontal cortex in the rat. *Brain Res.* 217:150–154, 1981.

Swanson, L. W., and Cowan, W. M. An autoradiographic study of the organization of the efferent connections of the hippocampal formation in the rat. *J. Comp. Neurol.* 172:49–84, 1977.

80    Gary Lynch

Swanson, L. W., Teyler, T. J., and Thompson, R. F. Hippocampal long-term potentiation: mechanisms and implications for memory. *Neuroscience Res. Prog. Bull.* 20:5, 1982.

Swanson, L. W., Wyss, J. M., and Cowan, W. M. An autoradiographic study of the organization of intrahippocampal association pathways in the rat. *J. Comp. Neur.* 181:681–716, 1978.

Tanabe, T., Iino, M., and Takagi, S. F. Discrimination of odors in olfactory bulb, pyriform-amygdaloid areas, and orbitofrontal cortex of the monkey. *J. Neurophys.* 35:1284–1296, 1975.

Tanabe, T., Iino, M., Ooshima, Y., and Takagi, S. F. An olfactory projection area in orbitofrontal cortex of the monkey. *J. Neurophys.* 38:1269–1283, 1975.

Thompson, R. F., Clark, G. A., Donegan, N., Lavond, D. G., Lincoln, J. S., Madden, J., Mamounas, J., Mauk, M., McCormick, D. A., and Thompson, J. K. Neuronal substrates of learning and memory: a "multiple-trace" view. In G. Lynch, J. L. McGaugh, and N. M. Weinberger (eds.), *Neurobiology of Learning and Memory*. New York: Guilford Press, 1984, pp. 137–165.

Tower, D. B. Structural and functional organization of mammalian cerebral cortex: the correlation of neurone density with brain size. *J. Comp. Neurol.* 101:19–51, 1954.

Tower, D. B., and Young, O. M. The activities of butyrlcholinesterase and carbonic anyhydrase, the rate of anaerobic glycolysis, and the question of a constant density of glial cells in cerebral cortices of mammalian species from mouse to whale. *J. Neurochem.* 20:269–278, 1973.

Toy-Oka, T., Shimuzu, T., and Masaki, T. Inhibition of proteolytic activity of calcium activated neutral protease by leupeptin and antipain. *Biochem. Biophys. Res. Comm.* 82:484–491, 1978.

Ulinski, P. Intracortical connections in the snakes *Natrix sipedon* and *Thamnophis sirtalis*. *J. Morphol.* 150:463–488, 1976.

Van Hoesen, G. W., Pandya, D. N., and Butters, N. Cortical afferents to the entorhinal cortex of the rhesus monkey. *Science* 175:1471–1473, 1972.

Van Valen, L. Theraspids as mammals. *Evolution* 14:304–313, 1960.

Vargas, F., Greenbaum, L., and Costa, E. Participation of a cysteine proteinase in the high affinity Ca2+ dependent binding of glutamate to hippocampal synaptic membranes. *Neuropharmacol.* 19:791, 1980.

Voronin, L. L. Long-term potentiation in the hippocampus. *Neuroscience* 10:1051–1069, 1983.

Weber, K., Shaw, G., Osborn, M., Debus, E., and Geisler, N. Neurofilaments, a subclass of intermediate filaments: structure and expression. 48:717–730, Cold Spring Harbor, 1983.

Welker, W., and Lende, R. A. Thalamocortical relationships in Echidna (Tachyglossus aculeatus). In S. O. E. Ebbesson (ed.), *Comparative Neurology of the Telencephalon*. New York: Plenum, 1980, pp. 449–481.

Wenzel, J., and Matthies, H. Morphological changes in the hippocampal formation accompanying memory formation and long-term potentiation. In N. Weinberger, J. McGaugh, and G. Lynch (eds.), *Memory Systems of the Brain: Animal and Human Cognitive Processes*. New York: Guilford Press, 1985, pp. 130–150.

White, J. G. Effects of an ionophore, A23187, on the surface morphology of normal erythrocytes. *Am. J. Pathol.* 77:507–518, 1974.

Whitfield, I. C. The object of sensory cortex. *Brain, Behav. and Evol.* 16:129–154, 1979.

Wigstrom, H., and Gustafsson, B. Facilitated induction of long-lasting potentiation during blockade of inhibition. *Nature* 301:603–605, 1983.

Wigstrom, H., Swann, J. W., and Andersen, P. Calcium dependency of synaptic long-lasting potentiation in the hippocampal slice. *Acta Physiol. Scand.* 105:126–128, 1979.

Willshaw, D. J., Buneman, O. P., and Lonquet-Higgins, H. C. Non-holographic associative memory. *Nature* 222:960–962, 1969.

Wilson, R. C., and Steward, O. Polysynaptic activation of the dentate gyrus of the hippocampal formation: an olfactory input via the lateral entorhinal area. *Exp. Brain Res.* 33:523–534, 1978.

Winson, J., and Abzug, C. Neuronal transmission through hippocampal pathways dependent upon behavior. *J. Neurophys.* 41:716–725, 1978.

Wong, R. K. S., Prince, D. A., and Basbaum, A. I. Intradendritic recording from hippocampal neurons. *Proc. Nat. Acad. Sci.* 76:986–990, 1979.

Woolsey, T. A., and van der Loos, H. The structural organization of layer IV in the somatosensory region (S1) of mouse cerebral cortex. The description of a cortical field composed of discrete cytoarchitectonic units. *Brain Res.* 17:205–242, 1970.

Wyss, J. M. Autoradiographic study of the efferent connections of entorhinal cortex in the rat. *J. Comp. Neurol.* 199:495–512, 1981.

Yarita, H., Iino, M., Tanabe, T., Kogure, S., and Takagi, S. F. A transthalamic olfactory pathway to orbitofrontal cortex in the monkey. *J. Neurophys.* 43:69–85, 1980.

Yokota, T., Reeves, A. G., and MacLean, P. D. Differential effects of septal and olfactory volleys on intracellular responses of hippocampal neurons in awake, sitting monkeys. *J. Neurophys.* 33:96–107, 1970.

Yoshimura, N., Kikuchi, T., Sasaki, T., Kitahara, A., Hatanaka, M., and Murachi, T. Two distinct Ca2+ proteases (calpain I and calpain II) purified concurrently by the same method from rat kidney. *J. Biol. Chem.* 258:8883–8889, 1983.

Zimmer, J. Ipsilateral afferents to the commissural zone of the fascia dentata demonstrated in decommissurated rats by silver impregnation. *J. Comp. Neurol.* 142:393–416, 1970.

Zimmerman, M., and Schlaepfer, W. W. Characterization of a brain calcium-activated protease that degrades neurofilament proteins. *Biochemistry* 21:3977–3983, 1982.

# Commentaries

The preceding paper used a particular type of synaptic plasticity and a set of hypothetical cortical networks as the mechanisms and sites of memory storage. The following commentaries consider these topics from three different perspectives.

Calcium-dependent modifications of postsynaptic structures were stressed in the paper, and possible presynaptic plasticities largely ignored. While this emphasis provided, it is hoped, some coherence to the arguments being advanced, it seems only appropriate that note be taken of the evidence that the axon terminal, and especially its transmitter chemistries, is modifiable. Ira Black describes here some recent illustrations of the surprising flexibility of transmitter systems and speculates on how these might be used to explain certain aspects of memory. New ideas about plasticity on the dendritic side of the synapse have also begun to appear. The possibility that dendritic spines have active membranes seems particularly pertinent to discussions of the links between synaptic changes and the operations of combinatorial circuits. This is the subject of the following comments by Gordon Shepherd. And then there is the issue of whether the combinatorial circuits, deduced from analyses of olfactory connections, might actually be found in the neocortex. This point is taken up by Herbert Killackey and placed in the context of past and present suggestions about the relationship of the functional neuroanatomy of cortex to memory.

Gary Lynch

# Apical Dendritic Spines of Cortical Pyramidal Cells: Remarks on Their Possible Roles in Higher Brain Functions, Including Memory

## Gordon M. Shepherd

There is general agreement that the cerebral cortex is of special interest with regard to memory mechanisms. However, one of the problems emerging in the discussions at this meeting is the difficulty of identifying the basic units of organization that provide for those mechanisms. There is clearly a need to characterize these units physiologically, anatomically, and biochemically, and identify them at the cellular and circuit level, in order to understand the principles underlying the psychological level of organization.

*The Basic Units of Cortical Function*

In addressing this question, I would like to focus on dendritic spines. Gary Lynch has already introduced us to the spine and some intriguing aspects of its biochemistry and physiology. We need to know as much as possible about the function of the individual spine, and we also need to understand better the functional context within which spines operate. This is part of the larger question of what precisely are the functions of the cortex. I would like to make some preliminary remarks about these questions, because I believe some traditional views are obscuring what are the basic units that underlie cortical function.

The traditional view is that cortical function depends on the inter-actions of many neuronal units, each neuron being represented by a cell body that acts as a simple summating device. The neuron sums several inputs and generates an impulse that travels in the axon to several sites of synaptic outputs. There is thus convergence of inputs, and divergence of outputs; all of us who work directly on neurons recognize this as a basic principle of neuronal organization. I assume also that at the psychological level one has to believe in units like this, which combine different inputs and send their outputs to different sites, in order to build systems that can mediate behavior. This is exemplified of course in the cell assemblies of Hebb (1949), and is explicit in recent models of neural networks with content-addressable memory (Hopfield, 1982).

This simplest of neural units, consisting essentially of a soma and an axon, is rare to find in the nervous system. It is in fact approximated by certain autonomic ganglion cells, such as Ira Black has discussed in his talk, which have relatively limited dendrites. However, most neurons have dendritic trees, which provide large surfaces for receiving synaptic inputs (and, in some case, sending synaptic outputs). Most neurons, therefore, are not simple summing devices.

The problem of understanding principles of cortical organization thus becomes heavily dependent on understanding the significance of the distal dentrites. One way to deal with this problem is simply to ignore it; in fact, the neuron is usually represented in pathways and networks devoid of its dendrites. However, as Wilfrid Rall (see 1977 for review) has shown, there is a significant spread of potentials within dendritic trees, which has forced neurobiologists to recognize that the dendrites must be taken into account in the final summation and integration of potentials at the site of impulse initiation at the origin of the axon (usually at the cell body). A basic problem, however, in assessing the dendritic input is that recordings are almost always from the cell body, and from the cell body the responses of the more distal dendrites often are weak and slow in the experimental paradigms used, and thus appear to have the nature of providing only slow background modulation. They have therefore traditionally been relegated to a secondary role in terms of the kinds of input-output relations of the neuron mediated by synapses at or near the cell body, which seem better placed to have an immediate and specific effect on impulse output.

In recent work with Rall as his collaborators, we have reassessed this traditional view of distal dendrites. It is in fact a seriously distorted view of the the true computational capabilities of the neuron, and represents very inadequately the organization of most neurons and the ways they carry out many of their functions. One way of putting a point on this is to say that, rather than the model neuron for most of the nervous system (including the cortex) being a neuron with most of its specific inputs located very close to the site of impulse output from the cell body, the strategy appears to be just the opposite, to site many specific inputs far out in the dendritic tree.

Why there should be this strategy is a question that, surprisingly, I believe no one has ever seriously addressed. It is a fact, however, that raises difficult problems in understanding the functions of distal dendrites. Part of the stimulus for pulling my thoughts on these problems together came from a conference that Francis Crick and I attended several years ago, at which he posed precisely this question. We have now at least a suggestive answer.

At this point we could make a survey of the nervous system, both vertebrate and invertebrate, comparing the types of dendritic inputs, but this would go beyond our time and relevance (see Shepherd, 1979, for review). Let me simply observe that in the retina, cerebellum, thalamus, and many other regions, the input fibers seem preferentially to make their synapses on the middle or distal parts of the dendrites. Since our interest is in the cortex, let us consider this point briefly with reference to the three basic types of cortex.

*Three Types of Cortex*

We start with the olfactory cortex. Gary Lynch has already provided us with an introduction to it, together with the rationale for starting here in thinking about the cortex. It contains a prototypical type of pyramidal neuron, with basal dendrites and an apical dendrite that has many distal branches covered with spines. All of the afferent fibers conveying information about the olfactory stimuli make their synapses on the spines on the most distal parts of the apical branches. Now you may say that this is a curious way to organize a system that has to detect and transmit specific information about different kinds of molecules at very low levels of concentration. Nevertheless, this pattern of connection is also expressed by the olfactory receptor neurons, which have their sensory transduction sites located distally on their dendritic tips and cilia, and in the olfactory bulb, where the receptor neuron axons make their synapses on the distal dendrites of mitral and tufted cells.

It may be noted that a similar pattern is present in other sensory systems. Photoreceptor cells, for example, transduce the light stimulus distally in modified cilia, and make their synapses on the distal processes of bipolar cells; and bipolar cells in turn make their synapses on the distal dendrites of ganglion cells. What we must recognize, therefore, is an important principle, that placement of synaptic inputs on distal dendrites is compatible with, and may in fact be optimal for, transmission and processing of specific information, even at low levels of signal intensity.

To what extent is this type of organization present in the hippocampus, which is part of the second kind of cortex, termed the archicortex? There is an obvious similarity in the projection of fibers from the entorhinal cortex to the distal apical dendrites of hippocampal pyramidal cells, as well as to the distal dendrites of dentate granule cells. This input, from a center for multisensory integration (the entorhinal cortex), may, by analogy with the olfactory cortex, be involved in more than just an overall modulation of background excitability of the pyramidal neurons.

What then of the neocortex? In Fig. 1A is shown, from Cajal, a typical pyramidal neuron, with basal dendrites, long apical trunk, and distal dendrites that branch and terminate in layer I. I think it is fair to say that, because of the traditional concept of the model neuron, virtually all attention with regard to input-output functions has been on the parts of the pyramidal neuron at or near the cell body; the distal dendrites, particularly in layer I, are largely unknown in terms of properties and functions, beyond the guess that they provide some kind of background modulation. In view of the long distances from layer I dendrites to cell bodies in deeper layers, even the background modulation has seemed destined to be very weak.

In order to assess the true functional properties, the true functional roles, of the spines, one needs to get inside them, just as one has had to get inside cell bodies and dendritic trunks to assess their functions. Ideally, this requires putting an electrode inside, or patching onto, a spine; unfortunately these techniques seem unfeasible, certainly in situ, in the foreseeable future.

## The Compartmental Modeling Approach

We have therefore approached this problem through modeling, building on the methods for compartmental analysis that Wilfrid Rall introduced in 1964 (Rall, 1964) in studies of the motoneuron, and that we applied at that time to olfactory bulb neurons (Rall et al., 1966; Rall and Shepherd, 1968). In that work we used a compartmental model, developed for tracer kinetic analysis; others subsequently have used programs written specially for a particular neuron model.

About 10 years ago, it occurred to me that there should be an easier way to do this, a way that would make this method more accessible for general application to any arbitrary neuron, by experimentalists who wanted to carry out modeling in parallel with morphological or functional analysis. The opportunity to do this came through a colleague at the IBM Watson Research Center, Robert Brayton, who had helped develop what is called in the trade an electrical network analysis program. This is used at IBM and elsewhere to construct electrical circuits and figure out ways of connecting components in order to obtain optimal output for a given input. Happily, it has all the elements one needs for modeling a nerve cell. We suggested for this purpose the use of a widely available program called SPICE, which is now being pursued

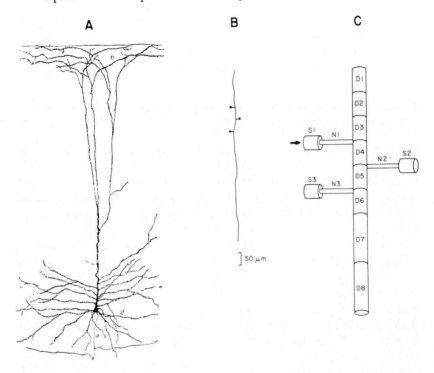

Figure 1
(A) Pyramidal neuron in the cerebral cortex; Golgi-impregnation (Cajal, 1911). (B) Schematic diagram representing the terminal segment of an apical dendritic branch in the most superficial cortical layer in A. Only three spines out of the total array are indicated, spaced 50 μm apart. This constitutes the system to be modeled. As can be seen by comparing with A, this model has a much smaller number of spines, with much greater spacing, than the actual case. (C) Diagrammatic representation of the compartmental model of B. Each compartment consists of a membrane capacitance (1 μmF/cm²) in parallel with a membrane resistance (2,000 cm²) and a voltage source for the resting membrane potential (−70 mV). The dimensions of each compartment are as follows: dendrites D1–D6, diameter 1 ;μm, length 50 μm; dendrites D7 and D8, diameter 1 μm, length 200 μm (D7 and D8 represent the extension of the branch toward the soma); spine necks N2 and N3, diameter 0.2 μm, length 3 μm; spine heads S1–S3, diameter 1 μm, length 2 μm. Each spine head includes a model for the nerve impulse, based on the Hodgkin-Huxley model (Hodgkin and Huxley, 1952). The arrow indicates that stimulation was by current injection into spine head S1. Similar results were obtained when stimulation was by an excitatory conductance increase.

in several laboratories (cf. Bunow, Segev, and Fleshman, 1985). In practice, as indicated in Figure 1, one divides the dendrite of interest into compartments, gives each its appropriate dimensions, and makes educated guesses about the ranges for relevant electrical properties.

## Passive Communication between Dendritic Spines

We started with a problem in the olfactory bulb: How is it that a synpatic response in one spine not only triggers synaptic output from that spine but also from neighboring spines (Rall et al., 1966)? I shall not go into that particular problem in detail, because it involves spines that are both presynaptic and postsynaptic. For present purposes the important point concerns the nature of the response within the spine. Judging the response from a recording site in the cell body, one expects it to be weak. However, the model shows that, instead of there being a small potential inside the spine, it has a large amplitude (Shepherd and Brayton, 1979). In fact, to produce the largest postsynaptic potential response for a given synaptic conductance change, this is exactly where that change wants to be located, in the smallest dendritic process of the neuron. By contrast, the smallest response for a given conductance change will be in the largest structure, the cell body, because of the large conductance load.

By virtue of these properties, a given synaptic input at the cell body gives rise to a very small synaptic potential; for a single quantum, this would be a "miniature EPSP" of 0.5 mV in amplitude or less (see Redman and Walmsley, 1983, for estimates of approximately 100 $\mu$V for a unit EPSP in a motoneuron). In a spine on a distal dendrite of a pyramidal neuron, however, that same quantum can produce an EPSP that is anything but "miniature"; with different estimates of quantal conductance, the EPSP can reach 40 mV or more, and even saturate. The reason, of course, is that the spine head, because of its very small size and narrow stem, has a very high input impedance. There is very little membrane for the current to cross; therefore, there is very large voltage drop across the membrane. By contrast, in the cell body, there is a large membrane area; the current density is low, giving a small voltage drop.

In addition to being of large amplitude, synaptic responses inside spines are, according to our simulations, temporally very precise. A 1-msec duration conductance change in a spine produces virtually a 1-msec duration spikelike transient potential (Shepherd and Brayton, 1979). The reason has to do with the small amount of membrane capacitance combined with the large amount of conductance loading through the spine neck; the current is continually drained away through the neck, so that the potential has a very rapid time course.

In summary, both of these properties of spine responses are counterintuitive to the view from the cell body; potentials generated in the spines are likely to have a large amplitude, and be temporally very precise.

What happens to this response when it spreads out into the dendritic branch? It spreads along the branch, limited by the passive cable properties of the membrane. At the same time, it spreads into neighboring spines situated along the branch. Our simulations showed that if there are output synapses on these spines (which applies in fact to a number of types of neurons in different regions of the nervous system), the transient is large enough and sharp enough to reach threshold for triggering a synaptic output. Thus, there is significant decrement of the potential in spreading *out of* the first spine head into the dendritic branch, but very little decrement in spreading *in to* the neighboring spines (Shepherd and Brayton, 1979; see also Rall and Rinzel, 1973). These kinds of considerations supported the concept, suggested many years ago, of the spine as an input-output device, which can have external inputs and outputs by means of synapses, internal outputs through the spine neck, and also internal inputs from the activity of neighboring spines (Shepherd, 1972). One also has the concept that the spine may have a threshold for some sort of output function.

A possibility that has occurred to us is that if there is an array of such spines along a dendritic branch, then with appropriate timing of synaptic inputs there would be a sequential biasing of the spine responses as one proceeded along the branch. There could thus be an enhanced response to a synaptic input closer to the soma, if that input was timed in such a way that the sequential biasing, by passive spread of the synaptic potentials alone, were to reach that spine at exactly the right moment (cf. Rall, 1964, for a similar argument applied to motoneuron dentrites). For example, a response spreading along a branch might raise the resting membrane potential of spine head by several mV, which would add accordingly to a synaptic potential in that spine. By this means, the responses in spines on distal branches could have specific effects in enhancing responses in more proximal spines. Our simulations thus suggest the principle that in any dendritic tree with spines, there will be significant input to a spine from its neighbors, and that with appropriately timed synaptic responses, this will provide a mechanism, by passive spread alone, of enabling distal synaptic inputs to have more immediate, specific, and stronger effects on cell output. This would appear to be built into any system in which there are linear arrays of spines and some degree of difference in timing of the inputs to those spines.

Many distal dendritic branches are very thin, and a question arises as to the extent of passive spread within them. The results of the simulations are counterintuitive in this respect as well: there is a surprising spread of potentials through very fine processes. If one examines an electron micrograph of central neuropil and sees a process that is less than a micron in diameter, one feels instinctively that a transient potential is not going to spread very far along it. In fact, by any set of reasonable assumptions, the electrotonic length of a process that is only 0.1 $\mu$m in diameter may be 100 $\mu$m or more (for calculations of this type, see Jack, Noble, and Tsien, 1975; Rall, 1977; Shepherd, 1979). Within that distance may be 50 or 100 spines or more. Thus, within the apical dendrite, synaptic responses are likely to be large and rapid, and spread effectively to neighboring spines by iterative passive spread between spines. There can thus be passive transfer of signals over considerable distances.

*Communication between Active Dendritic Spines*

Recently we have been interested in examining other possible properties of spines. Two laboratories—Wilfrid Rall's and Don Perkel's—have explored the possibility that spine heads may have active properties. They have both showed that if one puts the Hodgkin-Huxley model of the action potential into the spine head, it will generate an impulse in response to a depolarizing synaptic input (Miller, Rall, and Rinzel, 1985; Perkel and Perkel, 1985). The larger amplitude of the action potential greatly enhances the effectiveness of spread of responses from spines through distal dendrites.

The next step is obviously to analyze the communication between spines with these properties. There is at present a consortium of laboratories—Wilfrid Rall's, John Miller's, and my own—that are taking up various aspects of the problem (Shepherd et al., 1985). One of the basic types of model we are testing is illustrated in Fig. 1B,C (Shepherd et al., 1985). The morphological assumptions and cable properties for this particular example are indicated in the legend. The Hodgkin-Huxley model of the impulse is incorporated into each of the spine heads. The computational experiment consists of depolarizing the first spine to threshold, and testing whether the impulse will elicit further impulses in the spine heads farther along the dendrite. The only active membrane is in the spine heads: all other membrane, in the spine stems and dendritic branch, is passive. Note that this is different from the traditional idea, that if there is active membrane in a dendrite, it is probably near

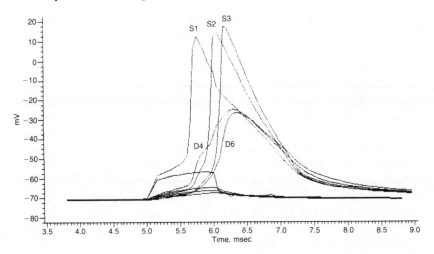

Figure 2
Saltatory impulse spread between spines in the distal dendritic spine model. A su-
prathreshold current pulse in spine head S1 elicits an impulse, which spreads passively
through dendritic segment D4 to trigger an impulse in spine head S2. This in turn spreads
through D5 to elicit an impulse in S3. Further spread into dendritic compartment D6
could elicit impulses in spines farther along the dendrite, providing the mechanism for
conveying the response of spine head S1 to the main apical dendrite and cell body.
Superimposed on the tracings are the small responses in each compartment to a just-
subthreshold current pulse in spine head S1. Note the all-or-nothing character of the
impulse responses in each spine head, and the conduction delays, which are equivalent
to a conduction velocity between S1 and S2 of 0.15 meters per second, and between S2
and S3 of 0.3 meters per second.

branch points of the main dendritic branches, where it serves to boost
activity along (Spencer and Kandel, 1961; Llinas and Sugimori, 1980;
Bernardo, Masukawa, and Prince, 1982). Our concern at present is with
the spines.

Under the above assumptions, a typical result is shown in Fig. 2.
This demonstrates the subthreshold response to a small injected current
in the first spine head; the threshold response to a slightly larger current;
the decrement in the spine as it spreads into the branch; and the generation of spikes in the second and third spines farther along the dendrite. Note that current is injected only into the first spine head; the
second and third spines generate impulses only in response to the
impulse spreading from the first spine. Because there is passive membrane everywhere except the spine heads, the impulse is not continuously propagated; it jumps from spine to spine in a way resembling
saltatory conduction in myelinated nerves.

By virtue of its morphological identity and these physiological properties, each spine may be regarded as a functional unit, interacting with other spine units. We suggest that this is precisely what is needed to enlarge the computational substrate of the cortex, in order to provide for higher brain functions such as memory.

One can next begin to assess the factors that will affect the communication between spines. In doing so, it is necessary to enlarge one's view of the spine unit, to include not only the synapse on the spine head and the spine head itself, but also the presynaptic part of the synapse, the spine neck, and some length of dendrite flanking the origin of the spine neck. These components together constitute a spine functional unit, the minimal unit for carrying out the essential input-output operations of a spine. Since there are both internal and external inputs, as discussed above, each spine functional unit operates as a semi-independent spine integrative unit.

### Active Spines as Functional Units Subject to Multiple Contingencies

A crucial feature of the spine unit is that its function is exquisitely dependent on virtually all its constituent components. Obviously, it is dependent on the synapse, and the amount and time course of transmitter released from the presynaptic terminal. It is dependent on the size of the spine head and molecular machinery within it. It is critically dependent on spine neck resistance. Rall and Rinzel (1971) suggested many years ago that changes in the diameter of the spine neck may provide a mechanism for memory through controlling the transmission of the synaptic response in the spine head. They emphasized that one has to take into account not only the spine neck, but the relation between the diameters of the neck and the parent dendritic branch from which the neck arises. The wider the dendrite, for example, the smaller the potential change within it. This factor by itself would appear to limit the amount of propagation that would take place as one moves through the dendritic tree toward the cell body. This would be counterbalanced, however, by other factors, such as confluence of potentials spreading from different branches, and synchronous activity in several spines so that their currents summate to activate spines farther along.

The spine, then, with its associated components, constitutes a unit of function. This is, I propose, the smallest unit underlying the integrative functions of the cortex. It is a mechanical and metabolic, as well as physiological, unit. It is a unit of function that fulfills the criterion of a computational unit that is subject to multiple contingencies, as is necessary for computations with the combinatorial complexity that Gary Lynch has pointed out in the olfactory cortex. The significance of having large numbers of spine units on distal dendrites is that it takes advantage of moving those synaptic inputs away from having an immediate, direct, obligatory effect on soma output, and making their effects contingent on specific combinations of inputs and cascades of nonlinear interactions between the spines.

For spines near the distal tips of the apical dendrites, the natural direction for spread of activity is toward the cell body. Within the dendritic tree, however, passive and active potentials spread in both directions, as in axons. Preferential spread toward the cell body would depend on factors that bias spread in that direction. In addition to the factors noted above, these might include an increase in membrane excitability, a more depolarized membrane potential, or differences in spine geometry. There is evidence that smaller spines, with thinner stems, tend to be found at more distal sites. However, if you try to pin down the people who are working on spines in different parts of the nervous system, most of them are very reluctant to talk about a representative spine size for different levels of a dendritic tree, because of the wide range of spine geometries. This wide range of spine shapes and sizes may in fact by very important; it could, for example, reflect ongoing dynamic changes in spine excitability properties dependent on frequency of synaptic input. Different spine shapes may thus reflect different stages of spine maturation.

Faced with the large numbers of spines present on the dendrites of cortical neurons, one may ask whether the activity of a single spine has any special significance in constituting a functional unit for higher brain functions. As neurophysiologists, we are accustomed to thinking of an individual synapse as making only a minute contribution to a recorded synaptic potential in a neuron such as a cortical pyramidal cell. Neurophysiologically, however, we work under artificial conditions when we deliver an electrical stimulus or sensory stimulus to an input pathway and excite a large number of fibers that make a synchronous input to the neuron we are recording from. During natural activity, conditions are likely to be much more complicated. First, there is likely to be some small proportion of the total number of input fibers active in any given natural state. Second, there is a probability of transmitter release at each synapse, a point usually neglected; one generally assumes that if an impulse invades an axon terminal, it always releases a quantum of transmitter. The work on active zones at the neuromuscular junction indicates that this is unlikely to be true; if, as at active zones, each synapse has a probability of release, that means that only a proportion (perhaps a few tenths) of the synapses in an active input array will release transmitter for a given presynaptic input. This suggests that, during natural behavior, a neuron is likely subjected to activity in a relatively small proportion of the synapses on it at any given time; this of course only increases the significance of the precise interactions between responses in individual spines in controlling the output of that neuron.

## Concluding Remarks

The above discussion has been concerned with only one aspect of distal dendritic function, the role of spines, and in particular the possibility of interactions between excitable spines. These studies have recently been extended by compartmental analysis of interactions that represent specific types of logic gates: AND, OR, and AND-NOT gates (Shepherd and Brayton, 1985, and in preparation; cf. Koch, Poggio, and Torre, 1982). The results indicate that these basic logic operations arise rather naturally out of interactions between excitable spines subjected to excitatory or inhibitory synaptic inputs with appropriate placement and timing.

These theoretical studies represent only one of several approaches that are presently being taken to analyze distal dendritic functions. With the recent cloning of the gene for the voltage-gated sodium channel (Noda et al., 1984), the use of monoclonal antibodies to identify sites of these channels in central neurons and their dendrites is not far off. The modeling results provide hypotheses that can be tested with these techniques. The methods may be difficult to apply, however, because of the likely low density of the voltage-gated channels in spines and problems of antibody specificity.

The Hodgkin-Huxley model has been used for the present analysis, but the presence of other types of voltage-gated channels seems equally, or perhaps more, likely. Electrophysiological studies of brain slices have provided evidence for the presence in dendrites of $Ca^{2+}$ currents (Llinas and Hess, 1976; Schwartzkroin and Slawsky, 1977; Llinas and Sugimori, 1980; Benardo, Masukawa, and Prince, 1982). Recently, it has been possible to begin to obtain direct evidence for the presence of $Ca^{2+}$ and $K^+$ channels in tissue culture using patch clamp recordings directly from dendritic branches of Purkinje cells (Gruol, 1983) and of hippocampal pyramidal neurons (Masukawa, Hansen, and Shepherd, 1985).

The information from all these approaches will have to be combined in order to construct a valid conceptual framework for interpreting the functions of distal dendrites and dendritic spines. The type of modeling discussed here can contribute to that goal by indicating some of the richness of computational substrate that could be available to the neuron in its distal dendrites. It will be intriguing to discover to what extent these possibilities are utilized for specific information-processing tasks in different types of neurons. Although the analysis is only beginning, it seems reasonable to postulate that the neural mechanisms underlying memory and related higher cortical functions will not be solved until an understanding of the functional properties of distal dendritic spines of cortical neurons is achieved.

## References

Benardo, L. S., Masukawa, L. M., and Prince, D. A. Electrophysiology of isolated hippocampal pyramidal dendrites. *J. Neurosci.* 2:1614–1622, 1982.

Bunow, B., Segev, I., and Fleshman, J. Modeling the electrical behavior of neurons with complex geometries and membrane properties using a network analysis program, 1985.

Cajal, S. Ramon y. *Histologie du système nerveux de l'homme et des vertebres.* Paris: Maloine, 1911.

Gruol, D. Analysis of voltage-sensitive ionic mechanisms mediating intrinsic activity of cultured Purkinje neurons. *Soc. for Neurosci. Absts.* 9:680, 1983.

Hebb, D. O. *The Organization of Behavior.* New York: Wiley, 1949.

Hodgkin, A. L., and Huxley, A. F. A quantitative description of membrane current and its application to conduction and excitation in nerve. *J. Physiol.* 117:500–544, 1952.

Hopfield, J. J. Neural networks and physical systems with emergent collective computational abilities. *Proc. Nat. Acad. Sci. (USA)* 79:2554–2558, 1982.

Jack, J. J. B., Noble, D., and Tsien, R. W. *Electric Current Flow in Excitable Cells.* Oxford: Oxford University Press, 1975.

Koch, C., Poggio, T., and Torre, V. Retinal ganglion cells: a functional interpretation of dendritic morphology. *Phil. Trans. Roy. Soc. Lond.* B298:227–264, 1982.

Llinas, R., and Hess, R. Tetrodotoxin-resistant dendritic spikes in avian Purkinje cells. *Proc. Nat. Acad. Sci. (USA)* 73:2520–2523, 1976.

Llinas, R., and Sugimori, M. Electrophysiological properties of in vitro Purkinje cell dendrites in mammalian cerebellar slices. *J. Physiol.* 325:197–213, 1980.

Masukawa, L., Hansen, A., and Shepherd, G. Single channel currents recorded from dendritic membranes of cultured dissociated neurons from the rat hippocampus. *Soc. for Neurosci. Absts.* 11:1183, 1985.

Miller, J. P., Rall, W., and Rinzel, J. Synaptic amplification by active membrane in dendritic spines. *Brain Res.* 1985.

Noda, M., Shimuzu, S., Tanabe, T., Takai, T., Kayano, T., Ikeda, T., Takahashi, H., Nakayama, H., Kanaoka, Y., Minamino, N., Kangawa, K., Matsuo, H., Raftery, M. A., Hirose, T., Inayama, S., Hayshida, H., Miyata, T., and Numa, S. Primary structure of Electrophorous Electricus sodium channel deduced from cDNA sequence. *Nature* 312:121–127, 1984.

Perkel, D. H., and Perkel, D. J. Dendritic spines: role of active membrane in modulating synaptic efficacy. *Brain res.* 1985.

Rall, W. Theoretical significance of dendritic trees for neuronal input-output relations. In R. F. Reiss (ed.), *Neural Theory and Modelling.* Palo Alto: Stanford University Press, 1964, pp. 73–97.

Rall, W. Core conductor theory and cable properties of neurons. In E. R. Kandel (ed.), *Handbook of Physiology,* Vol. 1: *The Nervous System.* Bethesda: Am. Physiol. Soc., 1977, pp. 39–77.

Rall, W., and Rinzel, J. Dendritic spine function and synaptic attenuation calculations. *Soc. Neurosci. Absts.*, p. 64, 1971.

Rall, W., and Rinzel, J. Branch input resistance and steady attenuation for input to one branch of a dendritic neuron model. *Biophys. J.* 13:648–688, 1973.

Rall, W., and Shepherd, G. M. Theoretical reconstruction of field potentials and dendrodendritic synaptic interactions in olfactory bulb. *J. Neurophysiol.* 31:884–915, 1968.

Rall, W., Shepherd, G. M., Reese, T. S., and Brightman, M. W. Dendro-dendritic synaptic pathway for inhibition in the olfactory bulb. *Exptl. Neurol.* 14:44–56, 1966.

Redman, S., and Walmsley, B. Amplitude fluctuations in synaptic potentials evoked in cat spinal motoneurones at identified group Ia synapses. *J. Physiol.* 343:135–145, 1983.

Schwartzkroin, P. A., and Slawsky, M. Probable calcium spikes in hippocampal neurons. *Brain Res.* 135:157–161, 1977.

Shepherd, G. M. The neuron doctrine: a revision of functional concepts. *Yale J. Biol. Med.* 45:584–599, 1972.

Shepherd, G. M. *The Synaptic Organization of the Brain*, second edition. New York: Oxford University Press, 1979.

Shepherd, G. M., and Brayton, R. K. Computer simulation of a dendrodendritic synaptic circuit for self- and lateral-inhibition in the olfactory bulb. *Brain Res.* 175:377–382, 1979.

Shepherd, G. M., and Brayton, R. K. Logic operations could be mediated by interactions between excitable dendritic spines. *Soc. for Neurosci. Absts.* 11:485, 1985.

Shepherd, G. M., Brayton, R. K., Miller, J. P., Segev, I., Rinzel, J., and Rall, W. Signal enhancement in distal cortical dendrites by means of interactions between active dendritic spines. *Proc. Nat. Acad. Sci. (USA)* 1985.

Spencer, W. A., and Kandel, E. R. Electrophysiology of hippocampal neurons. IV. Fast prepotentials. *J. Neurophysiol.* 24:272–285, 1961.

# Molecular Memory Mechanisms
## Ira B. Black

Our discussions were notably eclectic and wide-ranging, characteristic, perhaps, of a field attempting to define itself and emerge. Nevertheless, a number of central ideas were enunciated by this interdisciplinary group, allowing formulation of a provisional definition of memory at the molecular level. Indeed, general agreement that conceptualization at the molecular level is possible represents a heuristically valuable outcome. Consequently, concepts of molecular memory complement those of reverberating circuits, growth of new cell assemblies, neosynaptogenesis, and neurogenesis with ongoing neuronal turnover (Hebb, 1949; Horn, Rose, and Bateson, 1973; Tsukahara, 1981; Kandel and Schwartz, 1982; Thompson, Berger, and Madden, 1983).

Memory must involve the alteration of neuronal function and therefore requires *plasticity*, a change in state with experience. Moreover, mnemonic plasticity is characterized by (a) codification within the neuron, (b) short onset, (c) long-lasting effects, (d) specificity, (e) a high degree of precision, (f) enchanced effects with repetition, and (g) alteration of neuronal function. Further, mechanisms must allow for decay, or the phenomenon of forgetting. Finally, it was generally conceded that the synapse and its functions are likely to constitute a basic memory unit (Hebb, 1949).

Can we identify any synaptic components that undergo relatively long-term change in response to brief environmental stimuli and that, simultaneously, alter neuronal function? Do any synaptic molecules or molecular aggregates fulfill the foregoing criteria for a molecular memory system?

In fact, neurotransmitter functions, the agents of synaptic communication, undergo relatively long-term changes in response to brief experimental stimuli, and most definitely alter behavior. Transmitters and associated regulatory molecules encode, store, and express environmental information in a highly precise manner, thereby exhibiting mne-

This work was supported by NIH grants NS 10259, HD 12108, and NS 20788.

monic characteristics. Transmitter metabolism and even phenotypic expression are altered by discrete environmental stimuli. Relatively brief environmental events evoke long-lasting alterations in transmitter function, providing the *temporal amplification* that is central to mnemonic phenomena (Black, 1984). Transmitter metabolism and physiologic effects are *precisely* governed by specific regulatory molecules, many of which respond to environmental stimuli in a pattern characteristic of memory.

Further, it is now apparent that a single neuron may use multiple transmitters simultaneously, varying the actual transmitters employed, depending on environmental information (Black et al., 1984). The elaboration and use of multiple transmitters, many (if not all) of which are subject to environmental regulation, endows the neuron with plastic capabilities heretofore unsuspected. The expression, metabolism, and function of different transmitters in the same neuron are independently controlled by different regulatory molecules, each with distinct, characteristic time courses of action (for example, see Black et al., 1984; Adler, and Black, 1984). Consequently, even the single neuron can store information for *varying* periods of time, using multiple transmitter systems. Employing these systems alone, a single neuron may store immediate, short-term, and intermediate-term information (seconds to weeks), dictated by the *kinetics* of the regulatory molecules involved. Moreover, the apparent *combinatorial capabilities* confer degrees of *temporal specificity* and *precision* that have yet to be fully characterized.

It should be stressed that transmitters (and their regulators) are semantically as well as syntactically functional, an important attribute of memory molecules. As *the* synaptic signals, transmitters obviously alter communication and function. Consequently, transmitters are not simply indifferent or neutral storehouses of environmental information. Rather, environmental alteration of long-term transmitter function ipso facto alters function of the nervous system.

In summary, transmitters and their regulators fulfill many of the criteria for molecular memory systems.

## Specific Transmitters and Molecular Memory

Examination of several prototypical transmitters may illustrate the mechanisms available to perform memory functions, and may also indicate those functions unlikely to be subserved by transmitters. Approximately 50 individual amine, amino acid, purine, and peptide putative transmitters have already been identified, and the list is rapidly expanding. However, initially we focus on the catecholamine (CA) transmitters, since a great deal of relevant information has been derived from their intensive study over the past quarter of a century. Metabolism of individual transmitters is organized into relatively discrete, self-contained functional units. In the case of the CAs these units may be provisionally identified as (1) biosynthetic enzymes, (2) storage vesicles, (3) receptor apparatus, including associated second messenger, effector molecules, (4) the high-affinity neuronal reuptake inactivation mechanism, and (5) catabolic enzymes. (These units represent a minimum number, since each, in turn, may prove to consist of interdependent subunits.) These units do not appear to be directly independent and, in fact, are differentially influenced by intracellular and extracellular events.

It may be useful to examine one of the foregoing units in detail to illustrate mechanisms by which relatively evanescent environmental events elicit plastic responses in transmitter metabolism. CA biosynthetic enzymes have been studied intensively in mammalian sympathetic and central neurons and provide useful models. The sympathetic system, in particular, is well suited for this analysis, functioning at the interface of organism and environment, and playing a critical role in survival. The afferent, efferent, and central pathways of the sympathetic system transduce environmental demands into appropriate physiologic responses, ensuring integrated, adaptive behavior. The central role of the sympathetic system in the "fight or flight" reaction has long been recognized. How does environmentally induced enzyme regulation contribute to relatively long-lasting adaptation?

Environmental stress increases impulse flow in the sympathetic system, leading to changes in the activities of a number of CA synthetic enzymes through several discrete mechanisms. The net result of these effects is to increase flux across the biosynthetic pathway, with a consequent increase in available transmitter. Tyrosine hydroxylase (TH), the rate-limiting enzyme in CA biosynthesis, is of pivotal interest in this regard, simultaneously regulating CA synthesis, while responding to environmental stimuli (figure 1). TH, as an example, is subject to regulation through a number of mechanisms: feedback inhibition, enzyme activation, and biochemical induction. These different modes of regulation of this single molecule alter catalytic activity, and hence transmitter synthesis, over the span of seconds to minutes (inhibition and activation) to hours, days, and weeks (induction). Consequently, environmental events may specifically elicit functional transmitter changes over discrete time scales, constituting the molecular analogue of immediate, short-term, and intermediate-term memory.

TH is subject to feedback-inhibition by its products, dopamine and norepinephrine (figure 1; for review see Molinoff and Axelrod, 1971). Environmental stress increases the release of these amines, decreases

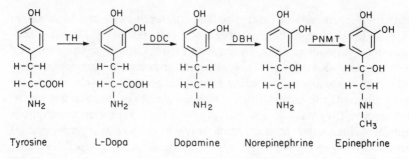

Figure 1
The catecholamine biosynthetic pathway. The biosynthetic enzymes are indicated above the arrows for each relevant reaction. Abbreviations used: TH, tyrosine hydroxylase; DDC, DOPA decarboxylase (L-aromatic amino acid decarboxylase); DBH, dopamine-β-hydroxylase; PNMT, phenylethanolamine-N-methyltransferase.

the cytoplasmic concentrations of the inhibitors, and results in the short-term increase in TH activity through disinhibition. In addition, increased impulse activity activates the enzyme, most probably through phosphorylation at multiple sites (Haycock et al., 1982; Meligeni et al., 1982), also resulting in elevated CA synthesis over seconds to minutes. While these mechanisms are relatively rapid, effects do persist for brief periods after the exciting stimuli are removed, thus constituting a form of short-term molecular memory. However, biochemical induction of the enzyme provides a mechanism for longer-term changes, and bridges the temporal gap from seconds and minutes to days and weeks.

A broad range of stressful environmental stimuli increases impulse flow in the sympathetic system, resulting in biochemical induction of TH (figure 2). Thus, for example, immobilization stress, cold stress, swimming stress, and treatment with pharmacologic agents that interfere with sympathetic function biochemically induce TH (Mueller, Thoenen, and Axelrod, 1969a,b; Thoenen, Mueller, and Axelrod, 1969a,b; Thoenen, 1970; Kvetnansky et al., 1971; Kvetnansky, 1973; Chuang and Costa, 1974). This *transsynaptic* induction is mediated by increased release of presynaptic acetylcholine, stimulation of postsynaptic nicotinic receptors with depolarization, and transmembrane sodium ion influx (see Bonisch, Otten, and Thoenen, 1980, for example). TH induction, as indicated above, increases the synthesis of norepinephrine. Consequently, environmental stress, through a series of well-defined molecular mechanisms, increases CA synthesis and release.

The physiologic sequelae of environmental sympathoadrenal activation are well documented and include an increase in cardiac output, generally an increase in blood pressure, elevated respiratory minute

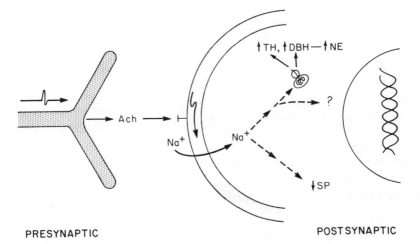

PRESYNAPTIC                                          POSTSYNAPTIC

Figure 2
Schematic diagram of the transsynaptic regulation of transmitter molecules in sympathetic neurons. Presynaptic impulses release acetylcholine (Ach), which interacts with postsynaptic nicotinic receptors, evoking transmembrane sodium ion ($Na^+$) influx. This sequence of events biochemically induces TH and DBH, resulting in increased synthesis of norepinephrine (NE) in the postsynaptic neuron. The same series of molecular events simultaneously decrease substance P (SP) and somatostatin (SS).

volume, mydriasis, piloerection, etc., components of the "fight or flight" reaction (Pick, 1970). In summary, then, well-characterized environmental conditions elicit reproducible neuronal functional changes that have been defined in detail at the molecular level. Are these functional changes long-lasting enough to be considered memory mechanisms?

In fact, the kinetics of TH induction have been analyzed in detail, and far outlast the inciting environmental stimuli. Stress and sympathoadrenal activation result in a 2- to 3-fold increase in TH activity in sympathetic neurons within 2 days, and enzyme activity remains elevated for at least 3 days after increased impulse activity has ceased. Moreover, direct, electrophysiologic nerve stimulation for 30–90 minutes increases enzyme molecule number for at least 3 days (Zigmond and Chalazonitis, 1979; Chalazonitis and Zigmond, 1980; Zigmond, Chalazonitis, and Joh, 1980). Consequently a brief stimulus evokes a long-term neuronal molecular alteration, providing the *temporal amplication* required of a neural memory mechanism.

## Repetition, Regulation, and Memory

Further, TH induction exhibits an additional property associated with mnemonic phenomena: repetitive stimuli elicit a progressive, incremental elevation of TH activity. For example, rats treated with the pharmacologic agent reserpine, which mimics environmental stress by increasing sympathetic impulse activity, exhibit TH induction (Mueller, Thoenen, and Axelrod, 1969a). Interestingly, a single injection causes a 2.5-fold increase in TH in 3 days, whereas repeated injections caused a 5-fold increase after 5 days. In analogous experiments, direct electrical stimulation of the preganglionic sympathetic trunk at 10 Hz for only 10 minutes increased enzyme activity by 25%, 3 days later, while stimulation for 60 minutes increased activity by 73% (Zigmond and Chalazonitis, 1979). To summarize, *repetition* and increased stimulus *duration* increase the magnitude of TH induction, as might be predicted for a molecular memory function.

## Transmitter Decay and Forgetting

The decrease in TH after induction has been analyzed in some detail and may serve to relate molecular decay and forgetting. Subsequent to induction, the half-time of decay is approximately 2 days, and normal basal levels of enzyme are attained 1 week after initial induction (Thoenen, Mueller, and Axelrod, 1970). The decrease in TH is mediated, presumably, by specific neuronal proteolytic enzymes, as in the case of other CA synthetic enzymes (Kessler et al., 1972; Ciaranello and Axelrod, 1973; Ciaranello, 1978). The salient point for the present discussion is that mechanisms of decay can be delineated in detail and may be directly relevant to the process of forgetting. For example, if degrading enzymes and potential inhibitors are defined in detail, it may be possible to approach forgetting pharmacologically. The present formulation provides a molecular basis for the common phenomenon of forgetting, whether due to faulty *retrieval* or *storage*. Characterization of the physiochemical aspects of the process of molecular decay may allow deeper insights and the evolution of new therapeutic approaches.

To epitomize, brief environmental events evoke relatively long-term neurotransmitter changes, consistent with mnemonic phenomena. Moreover, decay of enzyme activity after stimulation may provide an analogue of forgetting that can be analyzed in detail. On the basis of several criteria, consequently, these transmitter phenomena may constitute memory at the molecular level. One outstanding question, however, concerns the scale of the transmitter mechanisms under discussion. All of the studies cited have involved populations of neurons or single neurons, and none have been performed at the level of the single synapse. Methods for resolution at this level are not yet available. While it is plausible to envision enzyme disinhibition or activation at the single synapse, it is more difficult to anticipate how enzyme induction might be synapse-specific as opposed to neuron-specific. Nevertheless, the large number of regulatory mechanisms already described suggests that a variety of conditions may vary from synapse to synapse in the same neuron. For example, proteolytic, degrading enzyme concentration may vary from synapse to synapse, radically altering the consequences of TH induction at different synapses in the same neuron. In the absence of methods for direct measurement, however, such contentions remain highly speculative (see below for further discussion of synaptic specificity).

It must be stressed that in our search for likely memory molecules we have focused exclusively, thus far, on CA transmitters, within this category on synthetic enzymes, and, indeed, on a single critical enzyme, TH. We have completely ignored all of the other units of CA regulation, defined above, which may also be subject to environmental regulation. It is apparent that the potential for exquisite precision and specificity of synaptic communication is present within the apparatus of even a single transmitter. However, the recent realization that single neurons use multiple transmitters simultaneously (Hokfelt et al., 1980), and that the multiple transmitter status of a neuron is a dynamic state, influenced by the environment (Black et al., 1984), vastly increases the potential for precision and the variety of molecules available to serve memory mechanisms.

## Multiple Transmitters and Memory

Recent work has indicated that mature sympathetic neurons, long regarded as either noradrenergic or cholinergic, may, in response to appropriate environmental stimuli, express putative peptidergic transmitters such as substance P (SP; Kessler et al., 1983; Black et al., 1984). Denervation of sympathetic neurons in vivo, or treatment of rats with agents that block ganglionic transmission, increase SP dramatically (Fig. 2). Underlying mechanisms have been characterized in detail in tissue culture. Normally, mature sympathetic neurons exhibit a 10-fold increase in SP upon explantation to culture (and consequent denervation). However, exposure to depolarizing agents blocks the rise, and the effect of depolarization is prevented by tetrodotoxin. These observations indicate that depolarization, mediated by transmembrane sodium ion influx, normally suppresses SP in sympathetic neurons, an effect diametrically opposed to that on CA metabolism (see above; Fig. 2). The effects on SP last days to weeks. Thus, in the single neuron similar environmental events may be independently encoded in entirely different transmitter systems.

Recent work has raised the possibility that different transmitters may actually be localized to different cellular processes within the same neuron. SP, for example, is detectable in sympathetic neuron perikarya, and intraganglionic processes, but is undetectable in target organ terminals (Kessler, Bell, and Black, 1983). These observations raise the intriguing possibility that different synapses within the same neuron release different transmitters. A great deal of additional work is required to determine whether this is a widespread phenomenon. Nevertheless, specificity of different transmitters for different synaptic subsets in a neuron using multiple transmitters confers extraordinary combinatorial potential at the synaptic level. Such synaptic specificity conforms precisely to the demands of a molecular memory system, as indicated in the introduction, on the first page of this chapter.

The transmitter repertoire of the sympathetic neuron model is not restricted to catecholamines and SP: the same environmental stimuli that regulate SP similarly regulate sympathetic somatostatin (SS), another putative peptide transmitter (Kessler et al., 1983; Fig. 2). Since SS and SP are derived from different precursor polypeptide molecules, different posttranslational processes are probably involved in differential synthesis of the mature peptides. In turn, each would be expected to exhibit appropriate individual overall rate-constants for synthesis. It may be inferred that the multiple transmitter systems of a neuron encode environmental information for a spectrum of time scales.

These observations illustrate that a single physiological sequence, involving transsynaptic stimulation, postsynaptic depolarization, and transmembrane sodium ion influx, evoke long-term changes in multiple molecular species. Consequently, a discrete environmental event may be represented and stored in multiple molecules simultaneously. Thus, single neurons, and perhaps subsets of synapses of the single neuron, as indicated above, may represent a single experience in a variety of molecular forms.

Putative transmitters such as SP and SS, or transmitter regulatory molecules such as TH, function as symbols (Tomkins, 1975), coding for specific environmental stimuli. These molecular units of plasticity and transmitter function comprise an intraneuronal *representational system* in which symbol manipulations have physiological and behavioral consequences. This system interconnects several levels of function from environmental event to neuronal alteration to physiological response and behavior ("fight or flight"). Consequently, symbol manipulation in this system is semantically and syntactically functional, potentially altering the probability of survival. In this context, mnemonic molecular symbols simultaneously store environmental information and alter neuronal function. Molecular memory, therefore, is an integral part of normal neuronal function.

## Localization of Memory

The foregoing considerations suggest that questions concerning the "location" of memory within the nervous system may be improperly framed. Classification of "memories" on the basis of behavioral content, for example, working versus reference, declarative versus procedural, or episodic versus semantic, may help define functions of specific neural systems, but may confound content with process, and memory with multiple functions necessary for its expression. Analysis of the behavioral manifestations of memory should not introduce the unwarranted assumption that mnemonic mechanisms are restricted to neural subsystems most easily examined at the gross behavioral level. Detailed characterization of diverse behavioral functions in multiple neural systems may not necessarily define mechanisms underlying memory per se. Rather, molecular mnemonic mechanisms may be exhibited by a wide variety of neuronal systems that subserve very different physiological functions (e.g., see Black, 1984). Indeed, mnemonic function may represent a fundamental property of neuronal systems, whether peripheral or central.

## Summary and Conclusions

A number of summary statements concerning molecular memory may be warranted. First, temporal amplification of environmental stimuli through the induced persistence of altered molecular function is a form of memory itself, and not simply a "correlate." Second, different transmitter regulatory molecules exhibit different kinetics of activation, inhibition, and induction, depending on diverse genomic processes, tertiary molecular structures, and inactivation mechanisms, to cite several examples. Consequently, memories may be expected to span a temporal continuum, and not simply conform to classifications of "immediate," "recent," and "long-term." Third, the all-too-robust phenomenon of forgetting may be rigorously characterized by defining the kinetics of decay of specific molecular processes and species. Such information may even lead to the evolution of new therapeutic approaches to certain forms of forgetfulness. Finally, the general problem of memory localization within the nervous system may miss the point that a variety of neuronal systems exhibit mnemonic mechanisms.

While this discussion has focused on transmitter mechanisms exclusively, it is apparent that other molecules and mechanisms must also be involved in memory. Generally, transmitter changes are not quasi-permanent. Rather, transmitter functions return to normal, after long-term changes, resulting in a reset of the system to baseline. Although this confers a number of adaptive advantages, it does not account for memories lasting decades. It is certainly in this context that other mechanisms, including long-term potentiation (Lynch, 1985) and neosynaptogenesis, may be critical.

## References

Black, I. B. Intraneuronal mutability: implication for memory mechanisms. *Brain, Behav. and Evol.* 24:35–46, 1984.

Black, I. B., Adler, J. E., Dreyfus, C. F., Jonakait, G. M., Katz, D. M., LaGamma, E. F., and Markey, K. M. Neurotransmitter plasticity at the molecular level. *Science* 225:1266–1270, 1984.

Bonisch, H., Otten, U., and Thoenen, H. The role of sodium influx mediated by nicotinic receptors as an initial event in trans-synaptic induction of tyrosine hydroxylase in adrenergic neurons. *Naunyn-Schmied. Arch. Pharmacol.* 313:199–203, 1980.

Chalazonitis, A., and Zigmond, R. E. Effects of synaptic and antidromic stimulation on tyrosine hydroxylase activity in the rat superior cervical ganglion. *J. Physiol.* 300:525–538, 1980.

Chuang, D. M., and Costa, E. Biosynthesis of tyrosine hydroxylase in rat adrenal medulla after exposure to cold. *Proc. Natl. Acad. Sci. (USA)* 71:4570–4574, 1974.

Ciaranello, R. D. Regulation of phenylethanolamine N-methyl-transferase synthesis and degradation. I. Regulation by rat adrenal glucocorticords. *Mol. Pharmacol.* 14:478–489, 1978.

Ciaranello, R. D., and Axelrod, J. Genetically controlled alterations in the rate of degradation of phenylethanolamine N-methyltransferase. *J. Biol Chem.* 248:5616–5623, 1973.

Haycock, J. W., Meligeni, J. A., Bennett, W. F., and Waymire, J. C. Phosphorylation and activation of tyrosine hydroxylase mediate the acetylcholine-induced increase in catecholamine biosynthesis in adrenal chromaffin cells. *J. Biol. Chem.* 257:12461–12468, 1982.

Hebb, D. O. *The Organization of Behavior.* New York: Wiley, 1949.

Hokfelt, T., Johansson, O., Ljungdahl, A., Lundberg, J. M., and Schulzberg, M. Peptidergic neurones. *Nature,* 284:515–521, 1980.

Horn, G., Rose, S. P. R., and Bateson, P. P. G. Experience and plasticity in the central nervous system. *Science* 181:506–514, 1973.

Kandel, E. R., and Schwartz, J. H. Molecular biology of learning: modulation of transmitter release. *Science* 218:433–443, 1982.

Kessler, J. A., Bell, W. O., and Black, I. B. Interactions between sympathetic and sensory innervation of the iris. *J. Neurosci.* 3:1301–1307, 1983.

Kessler, J. A., Adler, J. E., Bell, W. O., and Black, I. B. Substance P and somatostatin metabolism in sympathetic and special sensory ganglia *in vitro. Neuroscience* 9:309–318, 1983.

Kessler, S., Ciaranello, R. D., Shire, J. G. M., and Barchas, J. D. Genetic variation activity of enzymes involved in synthesis of catecholamines. *Proc. Natl. Acad. Sci. (USA)* 69:2448–2450, 1972.

Kvetnansky, R. Trans-synaptic and humoral regulation of adrenal catecholamine synthesis in stress. In E. Usdin and S. Snyder (eds.), *Frontiers in Catecholamine Research.* New York: Pergamon Press, 1973, 223–229.

Kvetnansky, R., Gerwirtz, G. P. Weise, V. K., and Kopin, I. J. Catecholamine-synthesizing enzymes in the rat adrenal gland during exposure to cold. *Amer. J. Physiol.* 220:928–931, 1971.

LaGamma, E. F., Adler, J. E., and Black, I. B. Impulse activity differentially regulates leu-enkaphalin and catecholamine characters in the adrenal medulla. *Science* 224:1102–1104, 1984.

Lynch, G. This volume.

Meligeni, J. A., Haycock, J. W., Bennett, W. F., and Waymire, J. C. Phosphorylation and activation of tyrosine hydroxylase mediate the cAMP-induced increase in catechol-amine biosynthesis in adrenal chromaffin cells. *J. Biol. Chem.* 257:12632–12640, 1982.

Molinoff, P. B., and Axelrod, J. Biochemistry of catecholamines. *Ann. Rev. Biochem.* 40:465–500, 1971.

Mueller, R. A., Thoenen, H., and Axelrod, J. Increase in tyrosine hydroxylase activity after reserpine administration. *J. Pharmac. Exp. Ther.* 169:74–79, 1969a.

Mueller, R. A., Thoenen, H., and Axelrod, J. Inhibition of transsynaptically increased tyrosine hydroxylase activity by cycloheximide and actinomycin D. *Molec. Pharmacol.* 5:463–469, 1969b.

Pick, J. *The Autonomic Nervous System—Morphological Comparative, Clinical and Surgical Aspects.* Philadelphia: Lippincott, 1970.

Thoenen, H. Induction of tyrosine hydroxylase in peripheral and central adrenergic neurons by cold exposure of rats. *Nature* 228:861–862, 1970.

Thoenen, H., Mueller, R. A., and Axelrod, J. Increased tyrosine hydroxylase activity after drug-induced alteration of sympathetic transmission. *Nature* 221:1264, 1969a.

Thoenen, H., Muller, R. A., and Axelrod, J. Trans-synaptic induction of adrenal tyrosine hydroxylase. *J. Pharmacol. Exp. Ther.* 169:249–254, 1969b.

Thoenen, H., Mueller, R. A., and Axelrod, J. Phase difference in the induction of tyrosine hydroxylase in cell body and nerve terminals of sympathetic neurones. *Proc. Natl. Acad. Sci. (USA)* 65:58–62, 1970.

Thompson, R. F., Berger, T. W., and Madden, J., IV. Cellular processes of learning and memory in the mammalian CNS. *Ann. Rev. Neurosci.* 6:447–492, 1983.

Tomkins, G. M. The metabolic code. *Science* 189:760–763, 1975.

Tsukahara, N. Synaptic plasticity in the mammalian central nervous system. *Ann. Rev. Neurosci.* 4:351–380, 1981.

Zigmond, R. E., and Chalazonitis, A. Long-term effects of preganglionic nerve stimulation on tyrosine hydroxylase activity in the rat superior cervical ganglion. *Brain Res.* 164:137–152, 1979.

Zigmond, R. E., Chalazonitis, A., and Joh, T. Preganglionic nerve stimulation increases the amount of tyrosine hydroxylase in the rat superior cervical ganglion. *Neurosci. Lett.* 20:61–65, 1980.

# Morphology and Memory
# Herbert P. Killackey

It may seem presumptuous for a neuroanatomist to comment on phenomena that, at first glance, seem so far removed from what is usually considered to be the domain of neuroanatomy. However, I would point out that the morphology of the central nervous system, particularly in terms of the three-dimensional distribution of neurons and the interconnections between them, must be the physical substrate of the processes that we term memory. One can make the case that a major feature that distinguishes the central nervous system from other biological organ systems is the complexity of its morphology at the light microscopic level. Thus, I would submit that the unraveling of this complex morphology is relevant to an understanding of the processes that we term memory. However, it is equally clear that there are a number of psychological phenomena that are subsumed under the term memory. An understanding of these processes and their relationship to the physical substrate of the brain remains one of the greatest challenges confronting neurobiology.

It seems to me, and this conference reinforces this opinion, that we are at a stage where a good deal of effort can be devoted to the identification of candidate mechanisms and their relevance to processes of memory explored. In this light, two broad but interrelated themes have emerged from the current conference. The first of these themes concerns the site of lasting neuronal changes and the mechanisms by which such changes occur within the central nervous system. The second theme concerns the distribution of these sites within the central nervous system. At this conference, there was some consensus on both of these points. In terms of the first theme, the synapse in general, and the synaptic spine in particular, was proposed as the most likely site of lasting change. The second theme focused on the cerebral cortex as the structure most likely to play a preeminent role in memory processes.

The notion of the synapse as the site of lasting neuronal change is, of course, not a new one. One of the earliest and most influential expressions of this idea was that of Hebb (1949), who postulated that when one neuron repeatedly excites a second neuron, some lasting change takes place that increases the efficiency of the effect of the first neuron on the second. He went on to suggest that the most likely site of this effect was the synaptic knobs, which, with repeated firing, "develop and increase the area of contact between afferent axon and efferent soma." As Hebb himself pointed out, there was at this time no direct evidence to support his hypothesis; however, the current conference provided a good deal of evidence that supports a slightly modified version of this hypothesis.

While Hebb suggested that the site of change was in the synaptic knob or presynaptic specialization, most recent research has focused on a postsynaptic element, the dentritic spine. Current evidence suggests that changes in the dendritic spine may be regarded as candidate mechanisms for lasting neuronal changes. Lynch (this volume) has presented detailed evidence for this with regard to the hippocampus. I shall briefly summarize what I believe to be the most relevant points. First, brief bursts of high-frequency stimulation to an afferent input can lead to relatively long-lasting changes in the postsynaptic responsiveness of the target neurons (long-term potentiation). This is a direct demonstration of an increase in the efficacy of a neural circuit. Second, this functional change is accompanied by structural changes that include increases in the number of synapses and changes in the shape of dendritic spines. Third, Lynch has proposed that a relatively specific biochemical mechanism may underlie these changes.

In my opinion, such findings are very exciting and raise a number of interesting questions. While it seems unlikely to me that any such changes can be directly correlated with memory phenomena in the near term, they demonstrate the lasting modifiability of adult neuronal circuits under relatively specific conditions. Similarly, it remains to be seen what role such changes play in the still rather murky function of the hippocampus and whether such phenomena are restricted to the hippocampus or can be regarded as a more general feature of neuronal circuits. In this regard, as noted by Lynch, long-term potentiation can also be demonstrated in the neocortex (Lee, 1982), although the parameters of the phenomena in this structure have not yet been explored in detail. With regard to the specific biochemical mechanisms advanced by Lynch to account for these postsynaptic modifications, it was suggested by several participants that such biochemical changes were relatively rigid and irreversible and, hence, unlikely to play a role in processes that are as dynamic as memory. In this context, Black (this volume) pointed to another level of plasticity and neuronal interactions based on his studies of the developmental plasticity of transmitter types in autonomic ganglia that may have relevance to mechanisms of long-term neuronal change.

The question of the molecular basis of neuronal change has been addressed recently in a more general context by one of the participants at the meeting (Crick, 1984). In Crick's opinion, the outlook for understanding the molecular basis of change at the synaptic level is an optimistic one. In principle, recent advances in molecular biology have now made this a solvable problem and one on which the field of molecular biology should soon have major impact. However, I would submit that even if this is the case, the much larger problem of co-ordinated and distributed changes in neuronal circuits that undoubtedly underlie many memory processes is not amenable to such an approach.

If the views of Hebb can be taken as a modern starting point for the search for the neuronal site of lasting change, then those of Lashley on the distribution of the elements of memory, or the engram, should also be mentioned. At the end of an extremely productive career, a large part of which was devoted to an attempt to isolate sites of specific memories, Lashley (1950) facetiously concluded that "I sometimes feel, in reviewing the evidence on the localization of the memory trace, that the necessary conclusion is that learning is just not possible." It is clear that such a view is an overly pessimistic one and, as has since been determined, one that was based on experimental designs that had limitations of which Lashley was not completely aware. However, several of the points on which Lashley based his case should be briefly mentioned, as they are particularly relevant to the current conference. First, Lashley felt he had demonstrated that associative areas of the neocortex could not be regarded as storehouses for specific memories. As outlined by Allman at the conference, our views on the cortical areas involved in the processing of visual information have undergone considerable evolution since the time of Lashley. The two or so visual areas regarded by Lashley as playing a role in visual discrimination in the rat have multiplied into a dozen and a half or so different areas in higher primates. Some of these areas seem to be involved in the processing of highly specific information. Allman pointed to the work of Gross (Gross, Rocha-Miranda, and Bender, 1972), who has reported neurons in the primate (that) are specifically responsive to the faces of conspecifics as one of the most remarkable examples of such specificity and one that probably has relevance to specific types of memory. Second, Lashley suggested that within a given cortical area, all regions were equipotential in terms of their ability to retain a learned habit. This is a point that bears on the apparent distributed nature of the memory process and, perhaps, to the organization and distribution of the fundamental processing units of the neocortex (a point that is addressed below). Third, on the basis of his estimates of neuronal numbers in the rodent visual system, Lashley suggested that each neuron must take part in a great number of memories, but felt that even speculation as to how such a process could operate was futile. In this regard, the presentation of Shepherd at the conference was particularly exciting and has the potential to add a new dimension to our understanding of cortical organization.

Shepherd (this volume) has pointed out that our view of the function of the neuron is almost entirely based on the soma and axon and has for all practical purposes ignored the dendrite, which constitutes by far the greatest surface area of most neurons. Such a bias may be particularly limiting in terms of the neocortex. If the theoretical work of Shepherd, which suggests that dendritic spines are capable of active propagation, can be empirically demonstrated, the potential substrate for information processing within the neocortex will be vastly expanded. For example, one of the most characteristic neurons of the neocortex is the pyramidal cell. It is the major, if not only, output neuron from the neocortex. This neuron is found in all cortical layers and has as its chief defining feature a long straight vertically oriented apical dendrite that in most instances reaches from the cell body to just beneath the cortical surface. Thus, this apical dendrite is of a varying length and, in the case of deep pyramidal cells, may be as long as several millimeters. The apical dendrite of such a pyramidal cell is thickly encrusted with dendritic spines. It has been estimated that a single pyramidal cell may receive in the neighborhood of thirty thousand contacts (Bullock, 1977).

It has been well documented that both the size of a pyramidal cell apical dendritic field and the distribution of spines on the apical dendrite can be modified as the result of environmental experience in both neonatal and adult animals. However, it should be emphasized that such changes are responses to relatively large environmental manipulations and cannot be regarded as specifically related to memory processes. Aspects of this literature have recently been reviewed by Greenough (1984), who makes an interesting distinction between the types of changes seen in the neonatal animal, which he terms experience-expectant, and those in the adult, which he terms experience-dependent. Briefly, the former are a result of environmental events that all members of a species are likely to undergo and seem to play a role in the "fine tuning" of the brain with respect to its sensory environment. Many of these changes appear to be accomplished by the elimination of an initial overproduction of neuronal elements. In contrast, experience-dependent changes characteristic of the adult provide a basis for individual plasticity based on the idiosyncratic experience of a species member. Greenough hypothesizes that such changes are accomplished by the addition of new neuronal connections between closely spaced neuronal elements by mechanisms such as long-term potentiation. Such a view suggests a maturational shift in the nervous system's response to experience from a global tuning of groups of neuronal elements to local synaptic change. It should also be pointed out that while much of the above has focused on the changes in postsynaptic elements, the formation of new synaptic elements, such as the addition of spines, implies active change in presynaptic elements as well. Finally, I would add that the identification of local specific synaptic changes in response to environmental change within the neocortex is at or beyond the capabilities of existing anatomical methods. It is a problem of the magnitude of locating the proverbial needle in a haystack.

The coupling of the finding that both the distribution of synaptic spines as well as their shape are modifiable by experience in the adult animal with the suggestion from neuronal modeling that dendritic spines have active membrane properties has two major implications. First, the possible reservoir for information storage is vastly increased. Second, mechanisms for the storage and modification of this information are at least conceptually approachable.

Another aspect of the vertical organization of the apical dendrite of the cortical pyramidal cell should also be emphasized in relationship to the present conference. It was suggested by Hinton on the basis of his neuronal modeling experiments that relatively simple theoretical neuronal circuits can be demonstrated to have properties that resemble memory. This is a point that to a certain degree has been taken up by Lynch (this volume) and amplified in his discussion of types of neuronal circuits and their bearing on memory processes. In this discussion, using the olfactory system as a model, Lynch stresses the role of combinatorial afferent circuits in memory processes. These are circuits in which there is a good deal of overlap of afferent input onto a set of target neurons. As noted by Lynch, in contrast to the olfactory system, the dominant input to the neocortex from the dorsal thalamus is characterized by a high degree of topographic order and by little overlap within a set of afferent terminations. In my opinion, while the afferent organization to the neocortex has not been perfectly characterized, it is unlikely that major afferent systems within the cortex with distribution characteristics similar to the olfactory system remain to be identified. The one afferent system to the cortex that does seem to have this combinatorial organization is the noradrenergic projection from the locus coeruleus (Morrison et al., 1978). However, it should be noted that the high degree of topographic organization is largely, if not entirely, confined to the horizontal plane and that it is the middle layers of neocortex that seem to play a major role in the initial processing of sensory information. The neocortex is also characterized by a vertical dimension. As mentioned above, it is along this vertical dimension that the apical dendrite of the cortical pyramidal neurons is distributed. Cortical pyramidal neurons, particularly ones in the deeper layers, have their apical dendrite distributed in such a fashion that they pass through stratas of input arising from different sources. Thus, the pyramidal cell apical dendrite may be the chief combinatorial element of the neocortex.

A major assumption that seemed to be held by many conference participants was that the neocortex plays a particularly important role in the memory process. While certain relatively specific aspects of this assumption were discussed above, I would also like to speculate briefly on several other anatomical studies that I believe may have a bearing, albeit somewhat vague, on the subject of memory processing.

The first of these subjects is the evolution of the vertebrate brain and the evidence for an increase in the information-processing capabilities of this organ. While discussions on this topic usually focus on intelligence, I would submit that they can be equally well cast in terms of memory. Given that the integrative activity of the nervous system can be regarded as operating not only in space but also over time, many aspects of its operations in the second dimension are related to memory processing and are likely to have been a major factor in brain evolution. The most thorough and penetrating analysis of the evolution of the vertebrate brain in recent years has been provided by Jerison (1973).

The summary and analysis of data presented by Jerison suggest that there have been several rather discrete steps in the increase in relative brain size during the course of vertebrate evolution. In general, the brains of mammals are larger than those of reptiles and amphibians relative to body size, while within the class mammalia, the brains of primates are relatively larger than the brains of other members of the class, and, finally, the brains of hominids are clearly relatively larger than those of other members of the order primates. The selection pressures that drove these changes are not clearly understood, but are probably not the same in each case. Jerison presents an interesting argument that the first of these shifts may be due to the nocturnal niche occupied by early mammals. The sensory requirements of such a niche probably emphasized olfaction and audition. These are both senses in which spatial information is coded centrally rather than peripherally as in the visual system, and consequently this probably played an initial role in the relative enlargement of the mammalian brain. With the later return of mammals to diurnal niches, a new emphasis would have been placed on the visual system, and its further evolution would be based on the cortical model of auditory and olfactory processing rather than on the reptilian visual system. This is a process that has been greatly elaborated in primates. Thus, a good portion of the increase in the brain size of mammals including primates can be reasonably assumed to be correlated with the central elaboration of sensory processing systems. However, this does not account for the still larger relative brain size of the hominids. The adaptive pressures leading to this increase in size are still not well understood and are rather speculative. Among the interrelated factors likely to have played a role in this process are the development of a predaceous life-style, manipulative abilities, and social and communicative behaviors. At a somewhat more speculative level, Jerison has suggested that the continued evolution of cortical sensory systems, particularly auditory and tactile systems based on the model of a cortical visual system, led to the formation of imagery, or the creation of a perceptual world, which serves as a model of the real world. The adaptive significance of such cognitive imagery is enormous. It expands our world from the present into both the past and the future. Further, it is a process to which memory, in the common usage of the term, is central.

A significant question that follows from the enormous expansion of the neocortex during the course of mammalian evolution is whether or not this expansion is accompanied by fundamental changes in the way information is processed by the neocortex. It seems likely that the brain of higher primates may have more discrete areas for the processing of information and hence more complex patterns of connectivity. This is a point that has been documented in several sensory systems (see Van Essen and Maunsell, 1983, for the visual system and Kaas, 1983, for the somatosensory system). However, the basic structural organization of the neocortex is relatively invariant across mammalian species. Indeed, a recent study has suggested that the absolute number of neurons in a small volume of cortex extending from the cortical surface to the white matter is invariant both across cortical areas and in species as diverse as mouse, cat, and man (Rockel, Hiorns, and Powell, 1980). The only exception to this finding is the visual cortex of primates, which has roughly over twice as many neurons as the other cortical areas measured in primates and over double that of all areas in the other species examined. It should be emphasized that this constancy of neuronal number across species is found even though the thickness of the cortical areas examined in the different species varied by a factor of over two.

In my opinion, this finding has several significant implications for our understanding of the role of the structural organization of the neocortex in information processing and storage. First, it suggests that the fundamental unit of information processing is quite conservative and has remained relatively unchanged in the course of mammalian evolution. Second, the number of neuronal cortical processing units has increased enormously in the course of mammalian evolution. The most overt sign of this increase is the complex pattern of gyri and sulci of the primate neocortex, which serves to increase enormously its surface area, and hence the number of processing units, within the constraints of a relatively unyielding skull perched at the top of an upright body. Third, the processing capabilities of a given cortical unit may have increased significantly. An earlier part of this discussion focused on the apical dendrite of the cortical pyramidal cell, and there it was suggested that these apical dendrites may be the chief combinatorial element of the neocortex. Here it should be noted that the increase in cortical thickness implies a significant increase in the length of these dendrites, particularly the ones of the deeper cortical layers. It is very likely that this increase also includes an increase in the number of dendritic spines and in the richness of axonal strata with which they come in contact. Thus, the combinatorial properties of the basic cortical unit may have been enhanced in the course of mammalian evolution. One can speculate that cortical changes in the horizontal plane may be more closely related to increases in the capabilities for processing sensory information, while changes in the vertical dimension are more closely related to the combining and storage of information.

In the foregoing discussion I have attempted to relate some broad aspects of the neuroanatomical organization of the neocortex to information storage capabilities that may be related to memory in a rather speculative vein. I would like to end on an even more speculative note. As I look back on the conference, one aspect that strikes me is that most discussion was devoted to the memory process, in terms of storage and not in terms of how stored memories are retrieved or recalled. Some aspects of this problem were touched upon by Olton in his discussion of strategies for relating behavioral research to the brain and by Luce in discussing constraints in the interpretation of psychophysical research. It was the opinion of Crick, based on the demonstration by Hinton that simple theoretical neuronal circuits have a "recall" property, that this was a problem that had in principle been solved. Other participants, particularly Festinger and Gazzaniga, felt that this is not the case. They felt that the problem of recall is central to an understanding of memory processes but has yet to be adequately addressed by neurobiology. In this context, reference to the human neuropsychological literature is directly relevant. This literature, as best typified by reports of the patient H.M., points to the bleakness of the human experience in the absence of normal memory processes, particularly recall. However, this literature gives little feeling for the enormous capabilities of human memory and the ways in which human experience is vastly enriched by memory processes. It is with a few comments on this richness that I would like to end.

As a counterpoint to this bleakness, I would refer to one of the most famous passages of modern Western literature, which occurs near the end of the Overture to the first volume of Proust's *Remembrance of Things Past*. In this passage Prouse relates how the taste and undoubtedly smells associated with a sip of tea swimming with the crumbs of a petite madeleine evoke the memories of all that is to follow. Certainly, this is one of the richest works of the human imagination, and one in which memory plays a central role. It is also one that, from a much narrower perspective, can be interpreted as suggesting that the chemical senses play a particularly important role in human imagery, a point earlier alluded to by Lynch (this volume).

I would also like to note, as Boorstin (1983) has recently pointed out, that until the modern era memory played a far more central role in human affairs. This is a role that was made somewhat superfluous with the invention of movable type and the ready accessibility of the printed word. Indeed, training in the art of memory was regarded as a major part of rhetoric and, as such, was one of the cornerstones of education from the time of Greek antiquity to the Renaissance. The methods and reported results of this art of memory have been well documented by Yates (1966). Before them, the simple modern-day mnemonics devised by medical students to ease the burden of ana-tomical nomenclature seem very pale. The central device in this system was the mental construction of a building in all its details. Depending on what was to be remembered, this mental construct could be as simple as a one-room chapel or as complex as a Gothic cathedral. An individual could then use a set of well-formulated rules to place objects related to that which was to be recalled within corners, niches, rooms, or other architectural details of the building. At some later time the individual could then take an imaginary stroll through the construct and have its contents available for use. I refer the reader to a recent biography of the Jesuit missionary scholar Matteo Ricci by Spence (1984) in which such a memory palace is clearly explicated and serves as a central unifying device for the biography.

Such an architecture of memory leaves me with two impressions. First, it suggests the extensive role of sensory imagery in the memory process, and, by extension, the role of the neocortex toward which most sensory information is directed. Second, I take delight in the notion of a complex architecture of memory being constructed within the framework of the exceedingly more complex architecture of the human neocortex.

120    Herbert P. Killackey

## References

Black, I. This volume.

Boorstin, D. J. *The Discoverers*. New York: Random House, 1983.

Bullock, T. H. *Introduction to Nervous Systems*. San Francisco: W. H. Freeman, 1977.

Crick, F. Memory and molecular turnover. *Nature* 312:101, 1984.

Greenough, W. T. Structural correlates of information storage in the mammalian brain: a review and hypothesis. *Trends in Neuroscience* 7:229–233, 1984.

Gross, C. G., Rocha-Miranda, C. E., and Bender, D. B. Visual properties of neurons in inferotemporal cortex of the macaque. *J. Neurophysiol.* 35:96–111, 1972.

Hebb, D. O. *Organization of Behavior*. New York: Wiley, 1949.

Jerison, H. J. *Evolution Of the Brain and Intelligence*. New York: Academic Press, 1973.

Kaas, J. H. What if anything is S-1? The organization of the first somatosensory area of cortex. *Phys. Rev.* 63:206–231, 1983.

Lashley, K. S. In search of the engram. *Symp. Soc. Exp. Biol.* 4:454–482, 1950.

Lee, K. S. Sustained enhancement of evoked potentials following brief high frequency stimulation of the cerebral cortex in vitro. *Br. Res.* 239:1369–1372, 1982.

Lynch, G. This volume.

Morrison, J. H., Grzanna, R., Molliver, M. E., and Coyle, J. T. The distribution and orientation of noradrenergic fibers in neocortex of the rat: an immunofluorescence study. *J. Comp. Neurol.* 181:17–40, 1978.

Rockel, A. J., Hiorns, R. W., and Powell, T. P. S. The basic uniformity in structure of the neocortex. *Brain* 103:221–244, 1980.

Shepherd, G. This volume.

Spence, J. D. *The Memory Palace of Matteo Ricci*. New York: Viking Penguin, 1984.

Van Essen, D. C., and Maunsell, J. H. R. Hierarchical organization and functional streams in the visual cortex. *Trends in Neuroscience* 6:370–375, 1983.

Yates, F. A. *The Art of Memory*. Chicago: University of Chicago Press, 1966.

# Participants

John Allman, Ph.D.
Division of Biology
California Institute of Technology
Pasadena, California

Ira B. Black, M.D.
Department of Neurology
Division of Developmental Neurology
Cornell University Medical College
New York, New York

Francis H. C. Crick, Ph.D.
Salk Institute
San Diego, California

Leon Festinger, Ph.D.
Department of Psychology
The New School for Social Research
New York, New York

Michael S. Gazzaniga, Ph.D.
The Cognitive Neuroscience Institute
New York, New York

Corey S. Goodman, Ph.D.
Department of Biological Sciences
Stanford University
Palo Alto, California

Geoffrey E. Hinton, Ph.D.
Computer Science Department
Carnegie-Mellon University
Pittsburgh, Pennsylvania

Herbert P. Killackey, Ph.D.
Department of Psychobiology
University of California
Irvine, California

R. Duncan Luce, Ph.D.
Department of Psychology and Social Relations
Harvard University
Cambridge, Massachusetts

David S. Olton, Ph.D.
Department of Psychology
The Johns Hopkins University
Baltimore, Maryland

Gordon M. Shepherd, M.D., Ph.D.
Section of Neuroanatomy
Yale University School of Medicine
New Haven, Connecticut

# ⅉ Bradford Books

W. V. Quine. THE TIME OF MY LIFE.

Irvin Rock. THE LOGIC OF PERCEPTION.

George D. Romanos. QUINE AND ANALYTIC PHILOSOPHY.

George Santayana. PERSONS AND PLACES.

Roger N. Shepard and Lynn A. Cooper. MENTAL IMAGES AND THEIR TRANSFORMATIONS.

Elliott Sober, editor. CONCEPTUAL ISSUES IN EVOLUTIONARY BIOLOGY.

Elliott Sober, THE NATURE OF SELECTION.

Robert C. Stalnaker. INQUIRY.

Stephen P. Stich. FROM FOLK PSYCHOLOGY TO COGNITIVE SCIENCE.

Joseph M. Tonkonogy. VASCULAR APHASIA.

Hao Wang. BEYOND ANALYTIC PHILOSOPHY.